TEAM BOOTCAMP
EAT BETTER BIBLE

PALEO RECIPES & PRIMAL NUTRITION ADVICE THAT WORKS!

TEAM BOOTCAMP
EAT BETTER BIBLE

Tried & Tested Rapid Weight Loss
Recipes from the UK's Most Effective
Residential Bootcamp

TEAM BOOTCAMP
THINK, EAT & MOVE BETTER

TEAM Bootcamp
Eardington Manor
Bridgnorth
Shropshire
WV165JZ
team-bootcamp.com

Ordering Information:
Quantity sales. Special discounts are available on quantity purchases by corporations, associations, and others. For details, contact the publisher at the address above.

ISBN: 978-1-5272-4810-6 (pbk)

Contents

contents

contents

Acknowledgements

The *Eat Better Bible* would not have been possible without the support and assistance from the TEAM Bootcamp chefs and staff throughout the years. Each one has helped shape and structure the tried and tested nutrition programme delivered at Eardington Manor.

Paula & I would like to thank every member of the amazing TEAM Bootcamp staff and the hundreds of campers that make Eardington Manor an amazing working (and living!) environment. We are immensely proud of everything we do at TEAM and look forward to what promises to be an amazing future.

Finally, I would personally like to thank the single biggest reason I feel alive each day, my greatest ally, Paula. She deserves permanent and very public recognition for constantly greasing the wheels at TEAM Bootcamp and creating the perfect environment for people to thrive.

About TEAM Bootcamp

Launched in August 2013 by Paula & Craig Williams, TEAM Bootcamp quickly established a reputation for its rare combination of hard, no-compromise military-style training and soft, nurturing support. Based in Eardington Manor in Shropshire, TEAM has helped thousands of people Think, Eat & Move differently in pursuit of rapidly improved fitness, health and fat loss.

Since 2013, Craig, Paula and the life changing results at TEAM Bootcamp have been featured on the BBC, ITV, SKYtv, the Daily Mail, the Daily Telegraph, The Sun, Wired magazine and many more.

If you want to rapidly boost fitness and scorch calories in a relaxing and nurturing environment visit team-bootcamp.com or follow us on social media:

Facebook: @TeamBootcamp3d
Instagram: @team_bootcamp
Twitter: @Team_Bootcamp
Youtube: @Team Bootcamp

For daily tips, advice & behind the scenes insights into TEAM Bootcamp follow Craig on Instagram @Bootcamp_Craig.

Foreword

Since starting my journey at TEAM I've been through many roles, first as a client then an Ambassador and now as one of the chefs.

Having had a background in catering and hospitality Paula and Craig where keen to help me deal with my issues with food through working with them and the chefs to develop the menu and create new exciting dishes for TEAM Bootcamp and weight loss, which I did happily and it helped rediscover my passion for food and cooking but in a much healthier mindset.

The recipes in this book are a mixture of great options that can be used in any setting, whether it is just for yourself to give you a kick start on your own weight loss journey or for a special dinner party these recipes are great!

Anyone who has been lucky enough to have stayed at TEAM knows what an incredible and in many cases life-changing place it is and I can personally vouch for that! So please enjoy these recipes because they come to you full of love, positivity, hope and of course flavour!!

Best wishes,
Ricci Mussi

Ricci Mussi

SECTION ONE

Introduction

If you are reading this then you may have participated in my nutrition seminars or workshops or have spoken to someone that has. Whichever it is, you have obviously made a conscious decision to change your image and get your health in shape.

The bad news: despite what many fad diets will have you believe, getting your weight in check can be quite a challenge. It will take some real, sustained effort and determination.

The good news is that this book contains all the information you need to get your lifelong journey off to a great start.

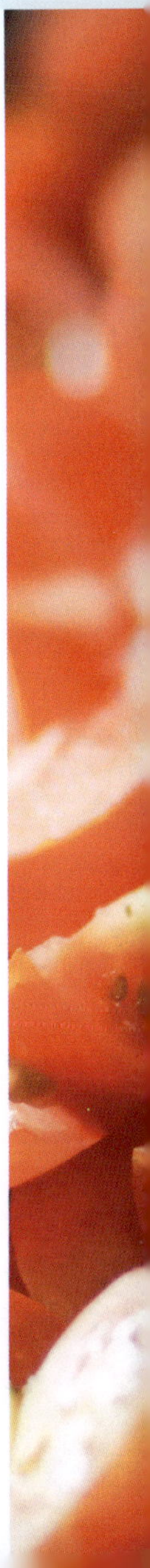

But, First a Little About Me

Paula, the TEAM and I coach hundreds to think, eat and move better at TEAM Bootcamp by infusing the lessons and strategies I developed through my own health and weight loss journey with the catering expertise of all the bootcamp chef's from throughout the years, but what about life before TEAM?

As a personal trainer, celebrity boot camp instructor and former Royal Marines Commando, you may think I naturally have a great body. The truth is that's not the case and I have been through the mill with regards to weight. Both Paula and I have and that's why we understand the physical and emotional highs and lows of carrying excess weight and having poor eating habits all too well. As a young marine, I got the nickname 'Pie Shop' and, while other recruits were given extra food, I was put on a calorie-controlled diet during training because of my 'rotund' appearance. That's a bit of a kick in the 'obvious' when you're supposed to be in the top 0.1 % of the fittest young men in the country!

Training for the Royal Marines is some of the most arduous in the world. It lasts 32 weeks and involves yomping, crawling and running mile after mile and jumping, climbing and swimming your way to an elite level of fitness, all whilst carrying 22lbs of kit and a rifle. Few people ever experience that intensity of the training, and I did it all when I was supposedly in my prime. So why was I still fat? Why was I embarrassed when I stood there in my budgie smugglers next to 45 other lads with chiseled bodies and washboard abs while I sported love handles and man boobs?

"Why, if I reportedly scorched 5,500 calories on an easy day in training, was I making myself sick in an effort to ditch the blubber, and why was I desperately seeking answers in one fad diet after the next?"

I wouldn't find the true answer to that for another 20 years . . . but when I did, my life changed forever!

Finding the answer was a long journey of study, trial and error and eventual discovery, but the good news is that eventually I got there. I cracked it and paleo nutrition was a large part.

Finally, I wish you the very best of luck, though wishing you luck suggests that you are leaving something to chance! To be honest, you are about to stack the odds in your favour with simple recipes that will rebalance your body and give you control over sugar, fast food and ultimately improve your health.

Craig Williams

AKA 'Pie Shop', and 3x world pork pie eating champ.

Eat Better Bible

At **TEAM Boot Camp**, we prescribe a paleo dietary plan, also known as the caveman or primal diet, which, if you don't know, reflects how our palaeolithic ancestors would have eaten pre-farming and before we started processing food. You will find an explanation of paleo below. For those that would like a deeper understanding, I recommend reading Robb Wolf or Loren Cordain, authors of *The Paleo Solution* and *The Paleo Diet* respectively.

In this section, we will teach you genuine weight loss principles to help you improve the WAY you eat, not what you eat.

Remember: don't try to change everything all at once! Start with some of the big hitters. For example, when I train I naturally and automatically want to eat cleaner. So creating the habit of training most days has made eating cleaner a by-product. These are known as keystone habits; take a few minutes to consider what some of your keystone habits are.

SOLID FOUNDATIONS

In order to succeed in your health and fitness goals, you are going to require three vital ingredients: sound nutrition, effective fitness training and sufficient rest. They seem obvious, but many people fail in their quest because they forget the words sound, effective and sufficient. Each component must be layered, starting with a solid foundation of sound nutrition.

Stop looking for the answer in the gym or in exercise.

You will never out-train poor nutrition. Exercise certainly forms some of the answer to your weight loss journey, but too much exercise can actually have a negative effect, especially if your training is ineffective.

TRIGGERS TO UNHEALTHY EATING

In my experience, there is rarely an occasion when a person makes a poor food choice where there hasn't been a 'trigger' of some form. An example is when you've had a terrible day at work and the last thing you want to do now that you are home is cook dinner. You grab the dog-eared takeaway menu and order the usual. You deserve a night off, right?

Identifying your own individual triggers is a major step in achieving your weight management goals. Learning to recognise the emotions, occasions or events that trigger unhealthy eating will immediately give you the upper hand.

During my time in the Marines, I learnt to identify 'combat indicators'. It was the only weapon we had against an unidentifiable enemy employing terror tactics rather than engaging in more traditional fighting. Combat indicators are the 'presence of the abnormal' or 'absence of the normal'. Every soldier is taught to recognise the slightest sign that trouble is brewing. Many lives are saved when the signs that something isn't quite right are noticed. It could be anything from displaced soil, indicating a buried explosive device, or the absence of civilians in a normally thriving marketplace, which could indicate the threat of a suicide bomber.

ACTION POINTS

Step one

Allocate a little time to consider your triggers to unhealthy eating. It is also helpful to catch yourself during your unhealthy eating periods to consider the situation, emotions, or events that led to poor choices.

Step two

Armed with your list of unhealthy eating triggers, consider all the ways to combat these triggers.

SLEEP YOURSELF THIN

Sounds too easy, right? You can make things significantly easier for yourself by understanding the body's natural reaction to crave sugary foods during the summer when the days are long and the nights are short. As cavemen, we evolved to crave food during the summer season when fruits, berries, honey and other natural sources of simple sugars were plentiful in order to fatten up for the cold, harsh winter months.

The problem comes in modern times. Our bodies are fooled into believing we are in a constant state of summer or a constant state of 'getting fat for winter'. The lights and heating allow us to treat night as day, unlike our ancestors, who would have been forced to wrap up for the night and sleep until dawn.

In order to use sleep and long nights to your advantage, aim for about 8–9 hours of sleep per night. That sounds like a lot, but, again, once we make better, more consistent, and effective sleep habitual, you soon develop the sleeping ability of a dormouse.

Additional benefits of sleeping longer include a reduction in the nasty bacteria that develop in the gut throughout the day and a reduction in cortisol levels (responsible for the storage of fat, particularly around the stomach and waist), which counteract the fat-burning hormone testosterone. You may feel sceptical about this, and you are right to feel that way. So I suggest that you try it or at least become more aware of what's happening in your body the next time you fail to get a good night's sleep. Mild effects include an increased desire for fast food, especially sugary, fatty and salty foods, and extreme effects can include gut irritation and ache owing to the build-up of bacteria and their waste products in the gut.

It is hard for many people to accept that the body does not get fitter, faster and leaner in the gym. It is during rest that the body repairs and recovers to become that little bit stronger and fitter in response to the stresses we placed on it through exercise. Viewing sleeping as healing rather than just sleep will help you to keep the importance of good-quality sleep in perspective.

The body repairs itself fully during the deep REM stage of sleep. This takes approximately 4 hours. Aim for 2 cycles of REM sleep per night to truly maximise your gains.

FOOD IS FUEL

With foods scientifically engineered to excite every taste receptor in our mouths, it is hard sometimes to remember that food is actually just two things: fuel and information.

This paragraph deals with the fuel aspect. In simple terms, every food has a determined amount of energy that will be absorbed by the body. If you eat more than you use, the body will convert a high percentage of the excess energy to fat to be stored in our fuel tanks: the hips, thighs, love handles and bingo wings!

FOOD IS INFORMATION

The body also uses food as information to control its basic functions, such as hormonal messages to get more sugar or say, "Stop eating — I am full." Improving your knowledge of the food groups, including knowing what each do and what information they provide, can significantly contribute to your ability to cope with and overcome cravings and prevent you from dropping well into the blood sugar 'crash zone'.

The great news is that all the recipes and the principles in this book will help feed the body with the right information, even without you realising it.

DISCIPLINE YOUR INSULIN

Insulin plays a huge part in the storage of fat, the use of energy in the body and the cravings for naff food. Learning to prevent erratic peaks and drops in your blood sugar levels and insulin can make weight loss and healthy living easier. I suggest reading *The Blood Sugar Solution* by Mark Hyman to learn all about the effects of food and the messages different ingredients send.

BALANCED MEALS

Though many of our basic processes slow at night, the body is constantly performing all the functions that keep us fit and healthy. These processes require nutrients that we obtain from food. Therefore, we need to ensure that the body has a constant supply of every food group throughout the day.

Over the next few weeks, develop a number of default meals containing optimal amount of protein, fats and carbohydrates for your body's requirements. Consuming balanced meals will ensure that you provide your body with everything it needs each time you eat.

Benefits of eating in this manner are the prevention of potential starvation periods, a boost in nutrient intake, the slowing of the digestion process as well as regulation of the fat storage hormone insulin.

Eating in a balanced manner is a little tough at first purely because we have been conditioned to eat carb-focused breakfasts, snacks and lunches and only make a concerted effort to include protein in our dinner.

What follows is an overview of the basic food groups and the functions they have in the body. If we know and understand what the food groups are, we can ensure that we always have balanced meals.

	CARBOHYDRATES	PROTEIN	FATS
What they do	Provide energy and control the release of insulin.	The basic building blocks of the body, utilised in the repair and rebuilding of tissue, organs and bone. Protein can also be used as energy in the absence of carbohydrates and fat.	Fats primarily provide energy for the body, but they also have more uses in the body than any other food group, including protection and the uptake of many vitamins and minerals. Interestingly, fats are a major component in every cell in the body, bones and the brain.
Your approximate amount	Aim for 2 fists of non-starchy carbs per major meal (i.e., breakfast, lunch and dinner) and 1 fist-sized portion for snacks and light meals.	Aim for a palm-sized portion of protein per major meal (i.e. breakfast, lunch and dinner). Half that amount for snacks and light meals.	Aim for a portion of fat roughly the size of the end of your thumb per major meal (i.e., breakfast, lunch and dinner) and half that for snacks and light meals.

WATER

Though water is not considered to be a food group, it is a great ally in your quest for cleaner eating and avoiding overeating.

What it does – Water is involved in almost every function in the body, but you can also fool your body's satiety signals by partially filling the stomach with water prior to eating.

Your approximate amount – Consume no less than 3 litres of water per day to prevent dehydration, the slowing of your metabolism and to help dispel hunger. In hot climates or on warm days, increase your water intake to compensate. As an indication, your urine should be a pale straw colour.

CRASH PREVENTION

We all know that feeling when we are so low on blood sugar that we are ready to kick the door off the fridge and bury our face in any sweet treat in there. Hitting the crash zone leads to one thing: the inability to make smart food choices! Avoid hitting the 'crash zone' with these three simple steps:

1. Eat regularly and aim for balanced meals every 2–3 hours to maintain blood sugar levels and prevent peaks and drops in blood sugar. Maintain breakfast, lunch and dinner as your larger main meals, but intersperse them with lighter meals which are smaller but have exactly the same balance of nutrients.

2. Recognise the early symptoms of a crash. The ability to recognise the onset of a crash can mean you head for the shops before it is too late and you simply cannot fight off the cravings for sugary, fatty and salty foods.

3. Predict when your blood sugar may start to waiver and prevent a crash by eating cleanly at the prescribed times to keep cravings at bay. Remember that when eating correctly,

you should rarely feel hungry and will often need to prompt yourself to eat as hunger and cravings are suppressed.

Today, poor choices are made incredibly easier. Crap food is usually cheaper, easier to get and is certainly more appealing owing to the most relentless marketing known to man. Make smart choices easy to make by creating cheap, easy-to-create default meals that you can fall back on as well as identifying smart snack choices in all your regular shops and cafes.

TACKLE SABOTAGE

There are two types of people in your life: those that will help you with your weight loss and fitness goals, called aiders, and those that will do EVERYTHING in their power to stop you! I call the latter saboteurs, and they are the enemy in your quest for a fitter, healthier and leaner you! They will try everything from pulling on your heartstrings to laying their own food- related guilt on you. Take a minute to consider who the saboteurs are in your life.

In my experience, the easiest way to tackle saboteurs is to confront them. I suggest the following:

> *"Mike, Tim, Sandra (or whatever their name is), as you know, I am trying to lose weight and get a little fitter, and I have identified you as a saboteur. You seem to go out of your way to prevent me from being truly happy with myself, and if you really did care about me, you wouldn't sabotage me you would help me."*

Then, pause for as long as it takes and wait to hear what they have to say for themselves.

PREPARATION IS KEY

Prior preparation and planning prevents piss-poor food choices. This takes little explanation, really. Planning and preparation are the keys to your success. Making a salad or grilling chicken for tomorrow takes time and effort, which, after a busy day at the office or running around after the kids, can be the last thing you want to do, but achieving your goals is going to take sacrifice and determination. You HAVE to plan ahead and prepare for the times you know that smart food is harder to get or inaccessible.

MAKE IT A HABIT

A very powerful thing to remember is the fact that it takes 21 days to form a new habit and a further 3 months to make that habit a lifelong change! Many people getting started on a fitness and fat loss programme fall off the wagon after 14 days or so because they take their eye off the ball. Just knowing that you need to push on for 21 days makes it much easier for you to succeed. It sets a target for you to meet, and once you reach it, things get that little bit easier.

SECTION TWO

Introduction

At **TEAM Boot Camp**, we prescribe paleo nutrition because eating as our ancestors did prior to farming will mean you are fulfilling all of the tips and advice in the previous section without having to think about it. This section will give you a basic introduction to paleo nutrition and highlight the accepted foods.

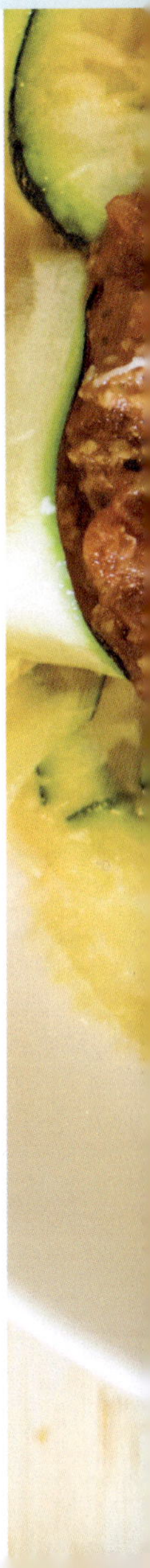

What to eat

The mantra of good paleo nutrition is to eat lots of lean meats, fresh vegetables, some fruits, nuts and seeds. In basic terms, if you can catch it, kill it and grow it, you can eat it, but as with everything, there are some exceptions to that rule.

Here are some basic guidelines for your primal eating :

Meats – Eat as much as you want for breakfast, lunch and dinner with no extravagant cooking methods. Stick to broiling, baking, roasting, sautéing and browning lightly, all with no or little-added fat. Drain off excess fat where possible.

When hungry or in doubt, lean meat is the most effective food group in reducing your appetite and boosting your metabolism to help burn stored fat.

Beef – Always trim any visible fat.

- Steak
- Lean burgers
- Top sirloin
- Veal
- Any other lean cut

Pork – Lean cuts only and always trim any visible fat.

- Pork loin
- Pork chops
- Any other lean cut

Poultry – White meat, skin removed.

- Chicken, ideally enriched omega 3 variety
- Goose
- Turkey breast

Offal

- Beef, lamb, pork and chicken livers
- Beef, lamb and pork tongues
- Beef, lamb and pork marrow
- Beef, lamb and pork sweetbreads

Other meats

- Rabbit
- Goat
- Game

Fish

- All unprocessed fish and shellfish, ideally wild caught

Eggs

- Chicken, ideally enriched omega 3 variety
- Goose
- Duck

Fruits and vegetables

Ensure you max out of fresh, non-starchy vegetables during each meal along with moderate amounts of nuts, avocado, seeds and unsaturated oils (flaxseed, canola, olive oil and mustard seed).

Limit fruit to one or two portions a day, and definitely do not eat bananas unless you train like a dog and need to replace energy quickly following a heavy training session.

Remember, not all vegetables are good. Avoid high-carbohydrate, starchy tubers, such as potatoes and yams, and restrict the amount of sweet potatoes to 1 or 2 a week.

Nuts are very energy dense. If you are trying to lose weight, you should restrict your nut intake to around 4 ounces a day. Every nut (except walnuts) are very high in omega 6, and excessive intake should be counteracted with high-strength fish oil containing a high dosage of omega 3 to balance the omega 6 to omega 3 ratio.

Dried fruit should be eaten in very small amounts because of the high glycemic load, causing a rapid increase in the blood sugar level.

Fruits

- Apple
- Cranberries
- Apricot
- Figs
- Avocado
- Gooseberries
- Blueberries
- Grapefruit
- Blackberries
- Honeydew melon
- Grapes
- Guava
- Cantaloupe
- Kiwi
- Lemon
- Cassava
- melon
- Lime
- Nectarine
- Pomegranate
- Orange
- Raspberries
- Papaya
- Rhubarb
- Passion fruit
- Star Fruit
- Peaches
- Strawberries
- Pears
- Tangerine
- Persimmon
- Watermelon
- Pineapple
- Plums

Vegetables

- Artichoke
- Mushrooms
- Asparagus
- Mustard greens
- Beet greens
- Onions
- Beets
- Parsley
- Bell peppers
- Parsnip
- Broccoli
- Peppers
- Brussels
- sprouts
- Pumpkin
- Cabbage
- Carrots
- Radish
- Cabbage
- Cauliflower
- Celery
- Seaweed
- Spinach
- Cucumber
- Squash (all kinds)
- Tomato
- Spring onions
- Kale
- Turnips
- Suede
- Watercress
- Lettuce

Nuts and seeds

- Almonds
- Pine Nuts
- Brazil nuts
- Pistachios
- Cashews
- Pumpkin seeds
- Chestnuts
- Sesame seeds
- Hazelnuts
- Sunflower seeds
- Macadamia nuts
- Walnuts
- Pecans

Foods you can eat in moderation

Oils

- Olive oil
- Avocado
- Walnut
- Flaxseed
- Canola
- Coconut oil

Drinks

- Coffee
- Tea
- Fruit juice

Other food

- Dried fruit

Foods to avoid

Avoid all processed foods and anything that starts with a capital letter, which suggests it's a brand name and not a real food.

Dairy products

- Butter
- Cheese
- Cream
- Milk
- Dairy spreads
- Powdered milk
- Yoghurt
- Ice cream

Cereal Grains

Avoid the following foods or foods that contain the following:

- Barley
- Corn
- Millet
- Oats
- Rice
- Rye
- Sorghum
- Wheat

Grain-like seeds

- Quinoa
- Buckwheat

Legumes

- All beans
- Black-eyed peas
- Chickpeas
- Peanuts
- Lentils
- Peas
- Sugar snap peas
- Peanut butter
- Miso
- Soybeans and all soybean products, including tofu

Starchy vegetables

- Cassava root
- Yams
- Tapioca
- Manioc
- Potatoes and all potato products

Foods high in salt

- Bacon
- Salami
- Processed meats
- Deli meats
- Pork rinds
- Frankfurters
- Cheese
- Ham
- Hot dogs
- Ketchup
- Pickled foods
- Olives
- Salted nuts
- Salted spices
- Sausages
- Smoked
- or dried fish and meat
- Virtually all canned meats and fish (unless you soak them)

Fatty meats

- Bacon
- Fatty cuts of beef
- Chicken or turkey legs, thigh, wings and skin
- Fatty cuts of pork
- Lamb chops
- Cuts of lamb

Soft drinks

- All soft drinks
- Energy drinks

Sweets

- All confectionary
- All refined sugars or foods high in refined sugar
- Cakes
- Biscuits
- Sweeteners
- Most honey

Breakfast

TQ121

4–6

20 mins

45 mins

Granola

INGREDIENTS

200g flaked almonds

200g chopped walnuts

100g pumpkin seeds

200g chopped macadamia nuts

200g chopped almonds

100g dried cranberries

100g sultanas

200g desiccated coconut

100g honey

2 tsp cinnamon

INSTRUCTIONS

1. Mix the chopped walnuts, macadamias, chopped almonds honey and cinnamon in a baking tray.
2. Bake in an oven for 12 mins at 160°c.
3. Remove and leave to cool.
4. Place the flaked almonds and pumpkin seeds in another baking tray and bake in an oven for 10 mins at 160°c.
5. Remove and leave to cool.
6. Once all the ingredients have cooled, place into an airtight container, add the coconut and cranberries.
7. Serve with unsweetened almond milk.

4 | 15 mins | 10 mins

Tomato, Bacon and Rocket Frittata

INGREDIENTS

1 small onion

4 plum tomatoes

4 slices of lean, unsmoked bacon

40g rocket

6 free range eggs

150ml of unsweetened almond milk

1 tsp olive oil black pepper

INSTRUCTIONS

1. Quarter the tomatoes and bake for 10 mins at 180°c
2. Slice the bacon into thin strips
3. Finely dice the onion
4. Heat the olive oil in a frying pan before adding the onions.
5. Add the bacon after a couple of minutes and cook for 5 mins before transferring to an oven dish.
6. Beat the eggs and milk in a mixing bowl along with pinch of black pepper.
7. Add the tomatoes, rocket to the oven dish before pouring the egg mix in and stirring.
8. Place in a warm oven at 180°c for 15 mins.
9. Slice into portions and serve with a small leafy salad.

4 | 15 mins | 15 mins

Avocado Poached Egg

INGREDIENTS

- 1 bay leaf
- 2 avocados
- 6 free range eggs
- 50ml extra virgin olive oil
- 1 lemon
- 1 tsp white wine vinegar
- Pinch of sea salt

INSTRUCTIONS

1. Half the avocado and remove the stones.
2. Place open face down on a baking tray and bake for 15 mins at 200˚c.
3. To make the sauce – Add the yokes of two eggs, vinegar, lemon juice and bay leaf together in a glass bowl on a Bain Marie and whisk for 30–60 seconds.
4. Pour in the oil whilst whisking until you have a good consistency, remove bay leaf and put sauce to one side.
5. Poach the 4 eggs in a pan of hot (not boiling) water with a splash of vinegar for 45 mins.
6. To serve place the egg on top of the avocado, flesh side up and drizzle with a little sauce.

4 | 6 mins | 10 mins

Bacon, Spinach & Red Pepper Omelette

INGREDIENTS

1 onion

4 slices of lean unsmoked bacon

40g of spinach

1 red pepper

8 free range eggs

Cracked black pepper

Pinch of sea salt

1 tsp olive oil

INSTRUCTIONS

1. Finely chop the onion, bacon and red pepper.
2. Beat the eggs and the black pepper together in a bowl.
3. Heat an omelette pan or small non-stick frying pan and sweat the onions.
4. Add the bacon and red pepper and cook, stirring occasionally for 45 mins.
5. Place the ingredients in a bowl and wipe the pan.
6. Add a small drizzle of oil to the pan and heat. Add ¼ of the bacon and pepper mix. Cook for 30 secs and then add ¼ of the egg mix.
7. Ensure the egg mix cooks evenly and after 30–40 secs, season with a pinch of salt and add 10g of spinach.
8. Fold the omelette. The heat of the omelette will continue to cook the egg and spinach slightly.
9. Plate and serve with a small leafy green salad.
10. Repeat with a further 3 omelettes

4 | 10 mins | 10 mins

Date & Honey Pancakes

INGREDIENTS

250g of arrow root – not Paleo, but worth it for pancakes

2 small free range eggs

150ml of unsweetened almond milk

60g of chopped dates

30g of Manuka honey

Pinch of sea salt

1 tsp olive oil

INSTRUCTIONS

1. Add almond milk, eggs and arrow root to a mixing bowl and whisk to an even consistency with no lumps or bumps.
2. In a hot non-stick frying pan, add a small ladle of the batter mix. Sprinkle with chopped dates and cook for 1 minute.
3. Flip and cook for a further 1 minute and serve.
4. Repeat for additional pancakes

4 | 20 mins | 20 mins

Smoked Haddock Florentine on Wilted Baby Spinach

INGREDIENTS

- 4 smoked haddock fillets
- 1 bay leaf
- 80g of baby spinach
- 6 eggs
- 50ml of extra virgin olive oil
- 1 tsp of white wine vinegar
- 1 lemon
- Cracked black pepper
- Pinch of sea salt
- 1 tsp olive oil

INSTRUCTIONS

1. To make the sauce – Add the yokes of two eggs, vinegar, lemon juice and bay leaf together in a glass bowl on a Bain Marie and whisk for 30–60 seconds.
2. Pour in the extra virgin olive oil while whisking and stir until you have an even consistency. Remove the bay leaf and place the bowl to one side.
3. Place the haddock on an oven tray, season with a pinch of salt and pepper and bake at 180°c for 10 mins.
4. In a hot pan, add the olive oil and spinach and stir for 2–4 mins until wilted. Season with salt and pepper to taste and remove from the heat.
5. Poach the eggs in a hot (not boiling) water with a splash of white wine vinegar for 4–5 mins.
6. To serve place the haddock onto the spinach with the eggs on top of the fish.
7. Finish with a drizzle of sauce over the egg and a pinch of black pepper.

Snacks

6 30 mins 30 mins

Cauliflower & Macadamia Humus

INGREDIENTS

1 large cauliflower

100g macadamia nuts

2 cloves of garlic

2 tbsp extra virgin olive oil

1 tsp cumin

1 lemon

½ tsp ground white pepper

¼ tsp paprika

INSTRUCTIONS

1. Boil or steam the cauliflower until soft and leave to cool for a few minutes.
2. Add the cauliflower and all the other ingredients to a food processor and blend until smooth.
3. Allow to rest in the fridge for 1 hour before serving.

6

45 mins

20 mins

Sesame & Cranberry Flapjack

INGREDIENTS

- 75g set honey
- 50g sesame seeds
- 100g dried cranberries
- 125g chopped walnuts
- 125 grams flaked almonds
- 75g sunflower seeds
- 100g chopped cashew nut
- 100g chopped almonds
- 1 tsp cinnamon

INSTRUCTIONS

1. Put honey, sesame seeds, walnuts, chopped and flaked almonds, sunflower seeds and cashew nuts in a pan and place on the stove on a low heat until honey has melted.
2. Add cinnamon and cranberries and fold in.
3. Put in a shallow tray lined with grease proof paper.
4. Bake at 150°C for 45 min.
5. Press with a similar sized tray and allow to cool.

4 | 20 mins | 25 mins

Chicken Nuggets

INGREDIENTS

1 tsp olive oil

2 chicken breasts

3 tbsps arrowroot

200g ground almonds

2 eggs

Cracked black pepper

1 lemon

Sage

INSTRUCTIONS

1. Cut chicken breasts into bite sized chunks.
2. Put the arrowroot, 2 eggs (beaten) and ground almonds into 3 different dishes for coating.
3. Zest ¼ lemon and add to almonds.
4. Add chopped sage and pinch cracked to almonds.
5. Coat chicken by putting it into the arrowroot and egg mix and the coat in the almond mix.
6. Place on a tray and leave in a fridge for 30 minutes.
7. With a hot pan add the oil and fry the nuggets turning them until they are a golden brown colour.
8. Put in the oven at 180°C for 12 minutes.

6

15 mins

20 mins

Chocolate Chip Cookies

INGREDIENTS

125g arrowroot

250g ground almonds

50g honey

2 eggs

50g 80 % or over dark chocolate (chopped)

INSTRUCTIONS

1. Mix all ingredients together thoroughly.
2. Roll the mix into 6 equally sized balls and press flat, about 7–8 mm thick
3. Line a tray with greaseproof paper
4. Bake at 170°C for 20 minutes
5. Allow to cool slightly so they firm up

4

10 mins

?? mins

Trail Mix

INGREDIENTS

75g whole almonds

30g chopped walnuts

30g chocolate cashew nuts

30g pumpkin seed

30g sunflower seeds

30g sultanas

30g chopped dates

INSTRUCTIONS

1. Mix all ingredients together, don't cook or bake.
2. Store in a sealed container in a dry place.
3. Serve approx. 55–65g per serving.

1 egg – 1 | 15 mins | 10 mins

Dark Chocolate & Pistachio Brownie

INGREDIENTS

20–30g rocket

4 eggs

Fresh chives or 1 tsp dried chives

¼ tsp cayenne pepper

½ tsp extra virgin olive oil

Cracked black pepper (pinch)

INSTRUCTIONS

1. Hard boil the eggs.
2. Place under running cold water until fully cooled.
3. Peel eggs and remove yolk and place in small bowl.
4. Add chopped chives, cayenne pepper, olive oil and black pepper to yolks and mix until smooth.
5. With a piping bag or tsp works the yolk mix back into the cooked egg white
6. Serve with rocket or salad (no dressing).

4 | 20 mins | 35 mins

Carrot Cake

INGREDIENTS

275g carrots

100g arrowroot

50g honey

1 tsp baking powder

50g ground almonds

2 tsps cinnamon

3 eggs

1 tbsp olive oil

INSTRUCTIONS

1. Grate carrots.
2. Put arrowroot, honey, baking powder, almonds, cinnamon in a bowl and mix.
3. Beat eggs in a separate bowl and add to mix.
4. Add grated carrot and olive oil and mix together.
5. Line a cake tin with greaseproof paper
6. Bake at 160°C for 25 minutes then at 140°C for 10 more minutes.

4

20 mins

7–8 hours

Coconut & Pineapple Pot

INGREDIENTS

600ml unsweetened almond milk

160ml tin of coconut cream

70g honey

5 gelatin leaves

100g pineapple pieces

INSTRUCTIONS

1. Put milk, coconut cream and honey in a pan on a low heat to warm through on the stove.
2. Remove from heat before it starts to boil.
3. While the hot mix cools for 10 minutes soak gelatin in cold water until soft.
4. Remove gelatin from water and squeeze out any excess water.
5. Stir the gelatin into milk mixture until dissolved.
6. Pour the mix into ramekins or small cups and place in fridge for 7–8 hours to set.
7. Allow to cool and garnish with pineapple pieces.

1 egg = 1

15 mins

10 mins

Chive & Cayenne Stuffed Egg

INGREDIENTS

20–30g rocket

4 eggs

Fresh chives or 1 tsp dried chives

¼ tsp cayenne pepper

½ tsp extra virgin olive oil

Cracked black pepper (pinch)

INSTRUCTIONS

1. Hard boil the eggs.
2. Place under running cold water until fully cooled.
3. Peel eggs and remove yolk and place in small bowl.
4. Add chopped chives, cayenne pepper, olive oil and black pepper to yolks and mix until smooth.
5. With a piping bag or tsp works the yolk mix back into the cooked egg white
6. Serve with rocket or salad (no dressing).

6 | 10 mins | 40 mins

Spiced Coconut Bites

INGREDIENTS

1 chicken breast

100g coconut milk yoghurt

1 tsp paprika

½ tsp cumin

½ tsp turmeric

1 clove of garlic

1 small green chilli

Small bunch of coriander

Pinch of cracked black pepper

1 baby gem lettuce

INSTRUCTIONS

1. Cook the chicken at 180°c in the oven for 20 mins then chill completely.
2. Finely chop the chilli and garlic and slice the chicken breast into thin slices.
3. Mix the coconut yoghurt, all the spices,garlic, chilli and a pinch of chopped coriander in a mixing bowl.
4. Add the chicken to the bowl and stir in.
5. Separate 6 leaves from the gem lettuce and wash.
6. Once dry, spoon on the chicken evenly between the leaves.
7. Finish with a pinch of black pepper and sprinkle of chopped coriander then serve.

4 | 10 mins | 30 mins

Feta and Basil Stuffed Tomatoes

INGREDIENTS

2 beef tomatoes

20g feta cheese

1 small shallot

1 clove of garlic

6 cherry tomatoes

1 tsp tomato puree

1 tsp olive oil

Small bunch of basil

Pinch of cracked black pepper

INSTRUCTIONS

1. Cut the beef tomatoes in half and spoon out the seeds.
2. Finely chop the shallot and garlic.
3. Quarter the cherry tomatoes and shred the basil.
4. Heat the olive oil and sweat the shallot and garlic for 3–5 mins.
5. Add the cherry tomatoes. Cook for 3 mins and then remove from the heat.
6. Stir in half the basil and spoon the mixture into each half of the tomato.
7. Crumble the feta on top and bake in the oven for 12 mins at 180°c.
8. Remove from the oven and allow to cool. Finish by sprinkling the remainder of the basil on top, season with black pepper and serve.

6 | 10 mins | 30 mins

Bacon, Tomato and Egg Muffins

INGREDIENTS

6 cherry tomatoes

4 eggs

2 slices of bacon

2 spring onions

1 bunch of chives

Pinch of cracked black pepper

1 tsp olive oil

INSTRUCTIONS

1. Slice the bacon, spring onion and chives.
2. Quarter the cherry tomatoes.
3. Crack the egg into a bowl and beat with a pinch of black pepper.
4. Heat a little oil in a pan and cook the bacon until crispy then add the spring onion and cook for 2 mins.
5. Put the tomatoes and chives into the pan, stir then remove from the heat.
6. Spoon the mixture evenly between 6 muffin cases.
7. Pour the egg mix evenly over each of the mixes.
8. Cook in an oven at 200°c for 15 mins and remove.
9. Allow to rest for 5 minutes before serving.

4

20 mins

20 mins

TEAM Bootcamp's Famous Chocolate Brownies

INGREDIENTS

½ cup plus 2 tbsps coconut oil

¼ cup cocoa powder

3 large eggs

½ cup plus 2 tbsps honey

1 tbsp vanilla extract

½ cup coconut flour

½ tbsp salt

⅓ cup chopped raw walnuts

⅓ cup mini dark chocolate chips.

INSTRUCTIONS

1. Preheat oven to 150°C and line an 8" × 8" glass baking pan with baking parchment leaving enough paper to overhang two opposite sides to help you lift it all out of the tray at the end.
2. In glass measuring jug melt the coconut oil in microwave and add it immediately to a large bowl with the cocoa powder and eggs and mix with an electric mixer until it is all combined.
3. Add the vanilla and honey before giving it another mix.
4. Now add the coconut flour and mix before mixing again. You've now finished with the mixer.
5. Fold in the nuts and dark chocolate and then transfer it all to the baking pan. Spread the mixture out evenly without knocking the air out of it too much. Basically be gentle!
6. Bake for 25–30 minutes or until a toothpick or skewer can be inserted into the centre and come away cleanly, e.g. no mixture sticks to it, or if you like a gooey brownie, minimal mixture sticks to it!
7. Cool your brownie creation on a wire rack and once it has cooled to room temperature cut it into squares. Store or freeze depending how many you need at a time.

4

15 mins

10 mins

TEAM Bootcamp's Coconut Cake

INGREDIENTS

½ cup coconut flour

½ tbsp baking soda

¼ tbsp sea salt

3 eggs

½ cup ghee or coconut oil

¼ cup full fat coconut milk

⅓ cup honey

2 tbsp vanilla extract

2 egg whites

Ghee or coconut oil for oiling pan

INSTRUCTIONS

1. Preheat oven to 175°C.
2. Oil a 9 inch round cake line and line bottom of pan with parchment paper by cutting a circle to fit the bottom on the tin.
3. In a large bowl, sift together coconut flour, baking soda and salt and set it to the side.
4. In another bowl, whisk together 3 eggs, fat of choice (ghee or coconut oil), coconut milk, honey and vanilla until it is foamy.
5. Add wet to dry and mix well to continue. Should this be put in paper cases?
6. Bake for 28–30 minutes, until toothpick or skewer can be inserted into centre and come out clean and cake is golden.

4 | 15 mins | 10 mins

TEAM Chocolate Chip Cookies

INGREDIENTS

100g almond flour

32g coconut flour

1 tsp baking soda

¼ tsp salt

84g coconut oil or butter

150g honey

98g almond butter

1.5 tsps vanilla extract

1 large egg

213g dark chocolate chips

INSTRUCTIONS

1. In a medium mixing bowl stir together the almond flour, coconut flour, baking soda and salt and set aside.
2. In a large mixing bowl with an electric hand mixer beat together the coconut oil or butter and honey at medium speed until well combined, this should take about 1 minute. If you use coconut oil it may not come together easily, if that's the case, use your hands to combine it and then beat another 20 seconds.
3. Beat in the almond butter and vanilla extract on medium speed and mix until combined. Beat in the egg on low and mix until well incorporated. Finally stir in 170g of the chocolate chips. Place the bowl in the fridge for about 1 hour or until the dough is firm.
4. Preheat the oven to 175°C and line a baking tray with parchment paper.
5. Roll the dough into balls and place the remaining 43g of chocolate chips on the top and on the sides of then dough balls. Place 3" apart on the prepared parchment paper. Press the dough balls down lightly with the palm of your hand. The dough will also expand when it cooks so give your cookies room to spread out!
6. Bake for 13–16 minutes or until the surface of the centre of the cookies no longer appears wet. They will be very soft but will continue to cook as they sit on the parchment paper.
7. Let cool completely on the parchment paper. Can be stored in an airtight container for up to 3 days.

20–24 | 15 mins | 10 mins

Sweet Vegetable Muffins

INGREDIENTS

6 tbsps of coconut oil

4 tbsps raw honey

12 large eggs

1 cup coconut milk

2 tsp vanilla extract

1 cup coconut flour

1 tsp baking soda

1 small tsp sea salt

1 courgette or carrot, finely grated

INSTRUCTIONS

1. Pre-heat your oven to 180°C and oil your muffin tins with coconut oil
2. This recipe is super simple! Chuck all ingredients in a large bowl and mix them thoroughly.
3. Spoon the mixture into your muffin tin/s so that it is evenly distributed.
4. Place try in oven for 15–20 min at 180°C, until you can place toothpick in centre of muffins and it comes out clean.
5. Allow your muffins to cool and store in an airtight container or freeze for another day.

4 | 15 mins | 10 mins

Paleo Pizza

(Yes you heard that right, pizza!)

INGREDIENTS

- 1 large egg
- 1 cup arrowroot powder
- ½ cup coconut flour
- ½ tbsp italian seasoning (dried)
- 1 tbsp sea salt
- ½ cup olive oil
- ½ cup water

INSTRUCTIONS

1. Preheat the oven to 450°C.
2. Combine the arrowroot powder, salt, Italian seasonings and ⅓ cup coconut flour in a bowl. Mix well.
3. Pour in oil and warm water. Stir. Add the whisked egg and mix until well combined.
4. Slowly add 2–3 tbsp more of coconut flour, one at a time, until the mixture is a quite sticky dough.
5. Put the dough on a surface sprinkled with arrowroot powder and gently need until it becomes a manageable ball that doesn't stick to your hands.
6. Place the ball on a sheet of parchment paper and using a rolling pin that has been dusted with arrowroot powder, roll the dough into a ¼ inch thick crust.
7. Place the dough, still not the parchment paper onto a pizza stone and bake for 12–13 minutes.
8. Remove the pizza crust from the oven, add toppings and cook for a few more minutes until the toppings are done.

4 | 15 mins | 10 mins

The Perfect Paleo Prawn Cocktail

INGREDIENTS

Natural full fat yoghurt

Garlic, chopped

Smoked paprika

Fresh lemon juice

INSTRUCTIONS

1. Mix, mix, mix. Serve!

4 | 15 mins | 10 mins

Ants on a Log

INGREDIENTS

1 stick of celery

1 tsp peanut butter

3 raisins

For alternatives try other nut butters and change to raisins for a chopped date, chopped dried apricot or other dried fruits you fancy. Just make sure they aren't bigger then 3 raisins.

INSTRUCTIONS

1. Chop the celery into finger length portions.
2. Infill the hollow of the celery with a slither of peanut butter and decorate with 3 raisins.
3. Allow two fingers of celery per portion.

4 | 15 mins | 10 mins

Baked Pears

INGREDIENTS

1 ripe pear

¼ tsp peanut butter

For an alternative version you can sprinkle with coconut, core the pear and add a blueberry, cherry or raspberry to its belly button hollow!

INSTRUCTIONS

1. Heat your oven to 180°C
2. Half the pear and spread with the peanut butter.
3. Pop in the oven of about 20 minutes.
4. Remember it will be very hot when it comes out of the oven and the peanut butter will stick to your mouth so let it cool a bit before eating it!

2p

29 mins

20 mins

Energy Balls

INGREDIENTS

2 cups dried fruit

2 cups nuts, seeds or shredded coconut

Use whatever combination of fruit and nuts or seeds you like. We often use 1 cup raisins, 1 cup dried apricots, 1.5 cups coconut and ½ cup almonds but the mix changes!

INSTRUCTIONS

1. Put everything in a food blender. If you're using dates or large dried apricots give them a whirl through the mixer before adding everything else. If not add everything and turn your mixed on.
2. You may have to stop the machine to move the mix around with a spatula before turning it back on to ensure it all mixes together.
3. Roll the mixture into walnut sized balls. It may feel grainy and like it won't stick together but give it a squeeze and it will hold together. If it doesn't add a little more fruit and mix again. To help with your portion sizes try using a tbsp measure to scoop up the mixture, this will also help you get it into ball shapes.
4. Alternatively you can flatten the mixture into a tray, pop it into the fridge to set and then cut it into energy squares
5. You can also roll the balls in coconut or drizzle with a little dark chocolate if you want. They can be frozen so you just need to defrost them as you need them.

4 | 15 mins | 10 mins

TEAM Bootcamp's Recovery Walk Flapjacks

INGREDIENTS

1 cup raisins

1 cup dried apricots

1 ½ cups shredded coconut

½ cup nuts

Alternative fruits, nuts and seed combinations will work too. Essentially you need 2 cups of dried fruit and 2 cups of nuts, seeds, coconut or whatever you fancy! Have fun experimenting and let us know how your creations turn out!

INSTRUCTIONS

1. Heat your oven to 180°C and line a tray with baking paper.
2. Put everything in a food blender. If you're using dates or large dried apricots give them a whirl through the mixer before adding everything else. If not add everything and turn your mixed on. (Don't worry if this all sounds very familiar, the first few steps are exactly the same as the energy balls!)
3. You may have to stop the machine to move the mix around with a spatula before turning it back on to ensure it all mixes together.
4. Tightly press the mixture into the baking tray and pop it into the oven for 25 minutes until it is golden and brown.
5. Take it out of the oven and let it cool slightly before portioning it up, don't leave it too long though or it will start to crisp up. 5 mins should be enough.
6. The flapjack can be frozen and defrosted when you need it.

4

15 mins

10 mins

Paleo Seed Bread

INGREDIENTS

3 cups almond flour

1 cup chia seeds

1 cup sesame seeds

2 cups pumpkin seeds

2 cups sunflower seeds

10 eggs

Pinch of salt

INSTRUCTIONS

1. Preheat oven to 170°C and line a 2lb loaf tin with baking paper.
2. Whisk the eggs before adding all of the other ingredients and mixing well.
3. Pore the mixture into the lined loaf tin, smoothing it slightly for an even bake.
4. Pop it in the oven for 45 mins
5. Once it is baked, let it cool before slicing it.

6–8 | 25–30 mins | 50–60 mins

Paleo Friendly Fish Cakes

INGREDIENTS

- 2 fillets of smoked haddock
- 150g of peeled and deveined prawns
- 2 fillets of any white fish (cod, Pollock etc.)
- 2 medium-large sweet potatoes
- finely chopped fresh chilli to taste
- 2 tsp chopped lemongrass
- 2 cloves garlic finely chopped
- 1 inch piece of fresh ginger, grated
- salt and pepper

INSTRUCTIONS

1. Place the sweet potatoes in a roasting tin with some olive oil and bake until soft.
2. Once cooled place the inside of the potato in a bowl with the herbs and spices and mix well.
3. Take the haddock and white fish and poach or roast for 10–12 minutes until cooked and allow to cool.
4. Dice up the prawns and add to the cooled potato, flake in the cooled fish and mix well.
5. Form the mix in to fish cakes on an oiled baking sheet, drizzle the top with olive oil and place in an oven at 180°C fan for 20–25 mins until hot all the way through and a crust has formed.
6. These can also be shallow fried or grilled.

20 | 10 mins | 15–20 mins

Mini Pizza

INGREDIENTS

- 20 slices of Chorizo or spicy salami
- 10 cherry tomatoes, halved
- 20 black olives
- 50g feta, cubed in to 20 pieces
- 1tbsp dried oregano
- 1tbsp dried basil
- 20 basil leaves

INSTRUCTIONS

1. Place the slices of chorizo or salami in to a mini tartlet/ canape tray.
2. Fill with half tomato, olive and feta, top with oregano and basil and bake for 10–15 mins at 180°C fan.
3. Serve with a fresh basil leaf whilst warm for best result.

Lamb

4

40 mins

120 mins

Rosemary & Garlic Lamb Steak with Aubergine and Courgette Stack

INGREDIENTS

- 4 lamb shanks
- 2 lt lamb or vegetable stock
- Bunch rosemary
- 1 bulb garlic
- 1 onion
- 2 carrots
- 1 lemon
- Olive oil
- 2 butternut squash
- 3–4 leeks
- 4 figs
- 35g honey
- Cracked black pepper
- Pinch sea salt

INSTRUCTIONS

1. Brown of the lamb shanks in a very hot large pan and move to a deep oven dish.
2. Roughly chop the garlic, onion, carrots and half the lemon.
3. Place into the oven dish with the lamb and add the stock and put in the oven at 180°C for 120 min.
4. Peel and dice the butternut squash into 1 cm pieces.
5. Slice and wash the leeks.
6. Quarter the figs and cover with the honey on an oven tray.
7. On a large oven tray add the butternut squash and leek season with a pinch of salt and pepper and a splash of olive oil.
8. Put in the oven for 45 min at 180°C.
9. Put the figs in the oven for 20 min at 180°C.
10. Once all is cooled serve with the vegetables on the bottom then lamb and finish with the figs and honey.

4 | 40 mins | 120 mins

Braised Lamb Shank on Roasted Butternut Squash & Leek with Honey Roasted Figs

INGREDIENTS

- 4 lamb shanks
- 2 lts lamb or vegetable stock
- Bunch rosemary
- 1 bulb garlic
- 1 onion
- 2 carrots
- 1 lemon
- Olive oil
- 2 butternut squash
- 3–4 leeks
- 4 figs
- 35g honey
- Cracked black pepper
- Pinch sea salt

INSTRUCTIONS

1. Brown of the lamb shanks in a very hot large pan and move to a deep oven dish.
2. Roughly chop the garlic, onion, carrots and half the lemon.
3. Place into the oven dish with the lamb and add the stock and put in the oven at 180°C for 120 min.
4. Peel and dice the butternut squash into 1 cm pieces.
5. Slice and wash the leeks.
6. Quarter the figs and cover with the honey on an oven tray.
7. On a large oven tray add the butternut squash and leek season with a pinch of salt and pepper and a splash of olive oil.
8. Put in the oven for 45 min at 180°C.
9. Put the figs in the oven for 20 min at 180°C.
10. Once all is cooled serve with the vegetables on the bottom then lamb and finish with the figs and honey.

4 | 30 mins | 90 mins

Paleo Lamb Tagine

INGREDIENTS

12 dried apricots

600g diced lamb

1 onion

2 cloves garlic

750ml lamb stock

2 medium chilli

1 tsp cumin

1 star anise

½ tsp cinnamon

2 cloves

1 red pepper

1 green pepper

1 tbsp tomato puree

Bunch coriander

1 butternut squash

50g macadamia nuts

1 tsp turmeric

INSTRUCTIONS

1. Using a hot pan brown the lamb and put in an ovenproof dish.
2. Finely chop the onion,garlic and chilli and sweat in the same pan and add to lamb.
3. To the lamb add the apricot, stock, cumin, star anise, cloves, cinnamon, turmeric and tomato puree, cover and put in the oven at 190°C for 25 min.
4. Peel and chop the butternut squash and slice the red and green pepper and add to the tagine, return to the oven for 60 min.
5. Once cooked finish with some toasted chopped macadamia nuts and chopped coriander.

4

30 mins

30 mins

Rack of Lamb, Sweet Potato Rosti, with Red Current & Thyme Sauce

INGREDIENTS

- 4 small trimmed racks of lamb
- 2 large sweet potatoes
- 2 red peppers
- 2 green peppers
- 1 can of artichoke hearts
- 100g red currants
- Bunch thyme
- 3 cloves garlic
- 1 tbsp arrowroot
- 1 tbsp olive oil
- 500ml lamb stock
- 1 tsp tomato puree
- Cracked black pepper
- Sea salt

INSTRUCTIONS

1. Peel and grate the sweet potato, add to a bowl with the arrowroot, pinch of salt and black pepper.
2. Form into 4 rosti's and squeeze out any liquid and let rest in fridge.
3. Roughly chop the red and green peppers and put in a tray with the artichoke, few sprigs of thyme, 3 crushed garlic cloves, oil and pinch black pepper and roast at 180°C for 35 min.
4. Pan fry the rostis and oven at 180°C for 30 min.
5. Using a very hot pan seal the rack of lamb and put on a try and season and cook at 180°C for 15 min and allow to rest for 6–9 min.
6. In the same pan deglaze with the stock, add puree, red currants and few sprigs of thyme.
7. Reduce the sauce to desired thickness and season with a pinch of salt and pepper.
8. To serve place the vegetables on a plate, slice the lamb between the bones and fan over, drizzle the sauce around and serve.

4 | 45 mins | 30 mins

Lamb Kofta with Tzatziki with Spiced Tomato, Shallots & Minted Cabbage

INGREDIENTS

2 tsp olive oil
600g lamb mince
2 medium onions
¼ cucumber
100g goats yoghurt
1 lemon
4 small bunches vine on cherry tomatoes
4 large shallots
½ white or red cabbage
Bunch mint
Bunch lemon thyme
Bunch coriander
1 tsp cumin seeds
1 tsp mustard seeds
2 medium chilis
½ tsp ground cumin
1 tsp paprika
1 tsp turmeric
1 tsp ground black
Pepper, Pinch salt

INSTRUCTIONS

1. Finely chop the onion, ½ chillies and small handful of coriander and add to lamb mince.
2. In a hot pan add cumin seeds, mustard seeds and cook dry for 4–5 min, cool and add to mince.
3. Add to the mince lemon zest, few sprigs of thyme,ground cumin, paprika, turmeric, pinch salt and pepper.
4. Mix the mince and form into 8 sausage shape kebabs and put on a skewer, seal on a hot pan and oven for 30 min at 180°C.
5. Peel and quarter the shallots, pan fry with some chili finely chopped and roast at 180°C for 20 min.
6. Slice the cabbage finely and add to a mixing bowl with 6–8 chopped mint leaves, 1 tsp olive oil, pinch of salt and pepper and juice of ½ lemon, mix and put in the fridge.
7. For the tzatziki, de-seed and finely dice the cucumber, chop 6–8 mint leaves and add to yoghurt with the juice of ½ lemon and pinch salt and pepper.
8. To serve, put the shallot and tomatoes on the plate and kebabs on top with the tzatziki spooned on the side.

notes

Beef

4

40 mins

120 mins

Braised Steak with Parsnip & Baby Onions

INGREDIENTS

- 4 × 6 oz rump or braising steaks
- 2 large parsnips
- 250g baby onion or baby leeks
- 500ml beef stock
- Bunch rosemary
- 3 garlic cloves
- 1 tsp olive oil
- 1 tbsp tomato puree
- Cracked black pepper
- Pinch sea salt
- Serve on its own or with sweet potato mash or seared savoy cabbage.

INSTRUCTIONS

1. Peel and roughly chop the parsnip.
2. Finely chop the garlic.
3. Using a hot non-stick pan seal of the steaks for 4–5 minutes on both sides in the olive oil.
4. Remove the steaks and put in an ovenproof dish.
5. Using the same pan put in the parsnips and baby onions and colour for 2 minutes and add to the oven dish with the steaks.
6. Add a few sprigs of rosemary and pour over the stock.
7. Add a pinch of black pepper and the tomato puree gently stir in.
8. Place in the oven at 180° C for 100 min.
9. Remove the rosemary stalks and then season with sea salt to taste.

4

60 mins

45 mins

Meatballs & Ribbon Vegetables

INGREDIENTS

Meatballs

600g lean steak mince

2 onions

Sage

2 garlic cloves

1 tbsp tomato puree

½ tsp ground nutmeg

Sauce

10 tomatoes or 2 tins chopped tomatoes

150g tomato puree

1 onion

1 celery stick

2 cloves garlic

1 tsp honey

Bunch basil

Pinch sea salt

Pinch cracked black pepper

Place the vegetables on a plate and spoon the meatballs on top.

INSTRUCTIONS

1. For the meatballs – Finely chop the onions and sweat in a pan until soft and allow to cool.
2. Finely chop the garlic and sage.
3. In a bowl mix the mince, onions, sage,garlic, tomato puree and nutmeg together and roll into bite sized balls.
4. For the sauce roughly chop the onion, celery and garlic and using a large pan sweat of for 10 min.
5. Add the chopped tomatoes, tomato puree and pinch of black pepper and simmer for 20 minutes.
6. To finish the sauce add the honey, stir and then blend until smooth.
7. Chop the basil finely and add to sauce with salt to taste. For the vegetables – Peel the butternut squash and using a vegetable peeler slice the butternut squash, carrots and courgettes.
8. Cook the meatballs in the oven at 200°C for 20 min and add to the sauce.
9. Heat a pan of water until boiling before adding the vegetables. Cook the vegetables for no longer than 90 secs.

4

29 mins

90 mins

Beef, Butternut Squash & Rosemary Stew

INGREDIENTS

500g diced beef

1 butternut squash

3 onions

1 leek

Bunch rosemary

750ml beef stock

2 carrots

1 tsp olive oil

1 tbsp tomato puree

3 cloves garlic

¼ tsp cracked black pepper

INSTRUCTIONS

1. Peel and dice the butternut squash into 1 cm pieces.
2. Chop the onion and carrot into 1 cm pieces.
3. Slice the leek and finely chop the garlic.
4. In a large hot pan brown of the beef in
5. the olive oil.
6. Add the onion,garlic, carrots, leeks and butternut squash.
7. Add the tomato puree, stock and 3 sprigs of rosemary and simmer for 80 minutes.
8. Once ready season with the black pepper to taste and serve.

4 | 50 mins | 90 mins

Beef and Spinach Chilli & Mexican Cauliflower Rice

INGREDIENTS

Chilli

300g lean steak mince
300g diced beef
2 onions
50g chopped jalapenos
3 medium chilli peppers
1 tbsp cumin
1 tbsp paprika
1 tsp mild chilli powder
1 tsp honey
125g tomato puree
400ml passatta

Rice

2 cauliflower
150g finely diced peppers
Bunch coriander
2 medium chillies
½ tsp turmeric
1 tsp olive oil

INSTRUCTIONS

1. For the chilli – Finely chop the onion and chilli peppers.
2. In a large hot pan, brown the diced beef and steak mince.
3. Add the onion and chilli peppers, cook for 10 more minutes.
4. Add the cumin, paprika, chilli powder and tomato puree and cook for a further 5 minutes.
5. Add the passatta and jalapenos, simmer for 60–70 min.
6. Add the honey and allow to simmer for a further 10 minutes.
7. For the rice – Finely chop or grate the cauliflower.
8. Finely dice the peppers and chillies.
9. Roughly shred the coriander.
10. Place the cauliflower, peppers, chilli and turmeric into an oven dish and drizzle with the olive oil.
11. Foil the dish and put in a preheated oven at 180°C for 25 min.
12. Remove from the oven and sprinkle the coriander and stir.
13. To serve put the rice on a plate and spoon the chilli on top, finish with chopped coriander.

4 | 45 mins | 80 mins

Beef, Butternut Squash & Rosemary Stew

INGREDIENTS

4 × 4 oz. rump steaks

2 onions

4 large flat mushrooms

Thyme

1 tbsp french mustard

12 baby leeks

3 sweet potatoes

3 cloves garlic

Parsley

1 tbsp olive oil

½ tspground black pepper

Pinch salt

800ml beef stock

1 tsp tomato puree

1 tsp arrowroot

INSTRUCTIONS

1. Using a tenderizer or rolling pin, put the steaks between 2 sheets of cling film as bash out until 3–4 mm thin.
2. Finely dice the onion,garlic and finely
3. slice the mushroom.
4. In a hot pan sweat of the onions, mushrooms and garlic.
5. To the mix add the mustard, a few thyme leaves, pinch black pepper and a little chopped parsley.
6. Stir on a low heat for 5 min and remove from heat and allow to cool.
7. Peel and roughly chop the sweet potato and boil for 25 min until soft.
8. Lay out the steaks and place the mushroom mix on evenly over the 4 and wrap the steaks around.
9. In a very hot pan seal of the olives and put in the oven and 180°C for 35 min
10. Top and tail the leeks and in a hot pan fry for 2–3 min and oven for 12 minutes at 180°C

4

40 mins

80 mins

Beef Olives, Braised Baby Leeks & Sweet Potato Puree

INGREDIENTS

4 × 4 oz rump steaks

2 onions

4 large flat mushrooms

Thyme

1 tbsp french mustard

12 baby leeks

3 sweet potatoes

3 cloves garlic

Parsley

1 tbsp olive oil

½ tsp ground black pepper

Pinch salt

800ml beef stock

1 tsp tomato puree

1 tsp arrowroot

INSTRUCTIONS

1. Using a tenderizer or rolling pin, put the steaks between 2 sheets of cling film as bash out until 3–4 mm thin.
2. Finely dice the onion,garlic and finely slice the mushroom.
3. In a hot pan sweat of the onions, mushrooms and garlic.
4. To the mix add the mustard, a few thyme leaves, pinch black pepper and a little chopped parsley.
5. Stir on a low heat for 5 min and remove from heat and allow to cool.
6. Peel and roughly chop the sweet potato and boil for 25 min until soft.out the steaks and place the mushroom mix on evenly over the 4 and wrap the steaks around.
7. In a very hot pan seal of the olives and put in the oven and 180°C for 35 min
8. Top and tail the leeks and in a hot pan fry for 2–3 min and oven for 12 minutes at 180°C

4 | 15 mins | 45 mins

Cottage Pie Topped with Sweet Potato Mash

INGREDIENTS

400g lean steak mince

1 large onion

2 carrots

1 leek

3 sweet potatoes

1 tbsp tomato puree

Thyme

400ml beef stock

Cracked black pepper

INSTRUCTIONS

1. Finely dice the onion and sweat off until soft and allow to cool.
2. Finally chop the garlic and chives.
3. Finely chop and wash the leeks
4. Peel and roughly chop the sweet potato and boil for 20 min
5. Using a hot large pan sweat of the onions and leeks, then add the carrots and mince
6. Add the tomato puree, thyme and beef stock and simmer for 20 min
7. Season to taste with black pepper
8. Put in an ovenproof dish and leave for 15–20 minutes
9. Drain and mash the sweet potato and neatly place on top of the mince filling, if you have a piping bag and nozzle pipe instead for a neater finish
10. Put in a hot oven at 200°C for 15 min then serve

4 | 60 mins | 180 mins

Slow Cooked Brisket with Roasted Veg & Almond Herb Dumplings

INGREDIENTS

Brisket

800g brisket
2 onions
4 carrots
2 clove garlic
1 ltr beef stock
1 tsp tomato puree
Rosemary
2 courgettes
2 red onions
1 butternut squash
Thyme
1 tbsp olive oil
125g arrowroot
300g ground almonds
Thyme
Parsley
1 tbsp olive oil
1 egg
2 tbsp cold water
Pinch cracked black pepper
Pinch sea salt

INSTRUCTIONS

1. For the dumplings – Place the arrowroot, almonds, thyme, chopped parsley, olive oil, egg, water, salt and pepper into a bowl and mix until a sticky dough.
2. Roll into 8 small balls and rest in the fridge.
3. For the brisket – Roughly chop the onions, carrots and garlic. Using a hot pan brown the brisket and put in an oven dish.
4. Brown the onions, carrots and garlic and place into the oven dish over the brisket. Add a few sprigs of thyme.
5. Using the same pan again add some of the stock to deglaze the pan and mix in the tomato puree, pour over the brisket. Cover with foil and put in the oven for 120 minutes at 190°C
6. For the roasted vegetables – Peel and cut the butternut squash into 1 cm pieces, chop the red onion and courgettes.
7. Coat the vegetables in the olive oil and add a few sprigs of rosemary and toss, put in the oven for 30–40 min at 190°C.
8. Remove the foil from brisket and place dumplings on top, cover again and return to the oven for a further 30 min before serving with the roasted vegetables.

2 10 mins 20 mins

Sirloin Steak with Mushroom and Plum Tomato

INGREDIENTS

2 6–8 oz sirloin steaks

1 large shallot

2 plum tomatoes

4 large flat mushrooms

Small bunch of thyme

2 tsp olive oil

Cracked black pepper

1 clove of garlic

INSTRUCTIONS

1. Heat 1 tsp of olive oil in a hot pan.
2. Slice the shallot and crush the garlic keeping it in one piece.
3. In the pan, fry the mushrooms then add the shallots and cook for 3 mins.
4. Add the tomatoes and a lot of thyme leaves, a pinch of black pepper and garlic clove.
5. Place in an oven at 170°c for 4 mins.
6. Rub the steaks with the remainder of the oil and a pinch of black pepper and cook on a hot griddle pan for 4 mins either side and allow to rest for 5 mins.
7. Serve on the tomatoes, mushrooms and shallots.
8. Can be served with sweet potato wedges and side salad.

4 | 15 mins | 15 mins | 10 mins

Beef Burger

INGREDIENTS

200g lean beef mince

1 onion

1 tsp paprika

1 tsp mustard

1 clove of garlic

1 tsp tomato puree

Small bunch of chives

Pinch of cracked black pepper

INSTRUCTIONS

1. To serve Paleo salsa
2. Paleo burger bun
3. Finely dice the onion and sweat off until soft and allow to cool.
4. Finally chop the garlic and chives.
5. Mix the mince, onion, paprika, mustard garlic, tomato puree, chives and black pepper in a bowl until evenly mixed.
6. Form the mixture into evenly sized balls and press into burgers. For best results allow to rest for a few hours.
7. Heat a griddle pan until very hot and cook the burgers. You may need to finish thicker burgers in the oven to ensure they are cooked thoroughly.
8. Serve with a salad and the salsa and paleo bun recipes available in this book.

TUSCAN
HERB
MEDITERRANEAN
HERBS INFUSED
Olive Oil
From SPAIN

2

25 mins

20 mins

Hearty Beef Stew

INGREDIENTS

Diced beef

Beef stock

Diced celery

Chopped onions

Chopped garlic

Fennel seeds

Arrowroot powder

INSTRUCTIONS

Slow cooker cooking:

1. Place all ingredients into a slow cooker and stir thoroughly.
2. Leave slow cooker on for 3–4 hours on medium setting stirring once every hour.

Oven Cooking:

1. Preheat oven to 100°C.
2. Place all ingredients in a large pot or glass tray, stir thoroughly.
3. Place pot or tray in oven at 100°C, leave in oven for 3–4 hours, stirring once every hour.

10 | 30–40 mins | 240+ mins

Bolognese

INGREDIENTS

- 2kg mince beef
- 2tbsp chopped garlic
- 3tbsp dried oregano
- 3tbsp dried basil
- 1tbsp dried rosemary
- 2 large onions finely diced
- 2 large carrots grated
- 3 sticks celery finely diced
- 2 tsp salt
- 1 tsp ground black pepper
- 3tbsp tomato puree
- 4 tins chopped tomato
- 1 litre passata
- 5 rashers streaky bacon (optional)

INSTRUCTIONS

1. Place the onions, celery, carrots, bacon and garlic in a hot pan and fry until onions turn translucent and begin to caramelise.
2. Add the mince and fry until browned.
3. Add your herbs and tomato puree salt and pepper and stir in.
4. Add you passata and tinned tomatoes and mix well turn down to low heat and let cook for minimum of 2–3 hours but it can be left all day just remember to stir occasional to prevent sticking.

Seafood

4 | 20 mins | 30 mins

Salmon Fillet on a Salmon Infused Medley of Fennel, Asparagus & Roasted Baby Plum

INGREDIENTS

4 medium sized salmon fillets

2 large whole fennel

12 asparagus spears

400g baby plum tomatoes

60g rocket

Bunch parsley

Bunch chives

Cracked black pepper

Pinch sea salt

Pinch saffron

2 tbsp olive oil

INSTRUCTIONS

1. Finely chop the parsley and chives.
2. Drizzle the tomatoes with ½ tsp olive oil and season with a pinch of salt and pepper.
3. Slice the fennel and trim the bottoms of asparagus and half them.
4. In a hot non-stick pan heat ½ tsp olive oil and put the salmon in skin down and put in the oven at 180°C for 12 min and nest for 5 min.
5. In a hot non-stick pan heat 1 tsp oil and put in the fennel and tomatoes stirring throughout for 3–4 min.
6. Add the asparagus, saffron, chives and juice of ½ lemon.
7. Finish with the rocket and take off the heat, season with a pinch of salt and pepper and serve.
8. Put on the vegetable mix and the salmon on to, skin side up as it should be crispy.
9. Garnish with chopped parsley.

4

35 mins

30 mins

Grilled Whole Plaice, Parmentier Sweet Potato, Pan Fried Kale and a Caper Lemon Sauce

INGREDIENTS

2 sweet potatoes

1 large kale

2 tbsp capers

1 lemon

Bunch chives

Bunch parsley

5 tbsp olive oil

1 egg yolk

1 tbsp white wine vinegar

Cracked black pepper

Pinch sea salt

1 small onion

1 clove garlic

INSTRUCTIONS

1. Peel and dice the sweet potato into 1 cm pieces and fry off in 1 tsp olive oil, chopped chives, juice of ½ lemon, pinch of salt and pepper
2. Put in the oven at 180°C for 30 min.
3. Heat a non-stick pan with 1 tsp olive oil and put in the plaice then into the oven at 180°C for 20 min, seasoned with black pepper and sea salt.
4. Finely dice the onion,garlic and parsley.
5. Slice the kale and pan fry in 1 tsp olive oil, pinch salt and pepper and let rest when cooked.
6. For the sauce use a metal or glass bowl over a Bain
7. Marie and whisk the yolk, vinegar, lemon juice and capers together, add the olive oil while whisking and remove from heat.
8. Sweat of the onions and garlic and add the sauce remove from heat and add parsley.
9. To serve put on the kale and potato with the plaice on top, pour over the sauce.
10. 4 whole plaice

4

35 mins

10 mins

Black Pepper & Almond Calamari with a Chilli & Lime Dip

INGREDIENTS

- 2 large squid tubes
- 60g arrowroot
- 1 egg
- 125g ground almonds
- 2 small chilli peppers
- 1 lime
- 50g goat's yoghurt
- Cracked black pepper
- Pinch salt
- 50ml olive oil

INSTRUCTIONS

1. Cut the squid into rings.
2. In 3 dishes put the arrowroot, 1 egg and almonds separate.
3. Add the peppers to the almonds.
4. Coat the squid in arrowroot then egg then almonds, put on a tray and chill for 1 hour.
5. Finely chop the chilli peppers and add to yoghurt.
6. Zest and juice the lime and add to yoghurt.
7. Season the yoghurt with a pinch of salt and pepper.
8. Heat up the oil and fry the squid for no more than 90 seconds.
9. Place on a tray when cooked and season with a pinch of salt.
10. Serve with the dip and can be served with side salad.

4 | 25 mins | 15 mins

Garlic & Chive Tiger Prawns, Savoy Cabbage Noodles & Cucumber & Horseradish Pickle

INGREDIENTS

- 600g tiger prawns
- 2 cloves garlic
- Bunch chives
- 1 lemon
- 1 tsp white wine
- 1 large savoy cabbage
- 3 tbsp olive oil
- ½ cucumber
- ½ fresh horseradish
- 50ml white wine vinegar
- ½ tsp fennel seeds
- ½ tsp mustard seeds
- 4 cardamom pods
- 1 mild chilli pepper
- Cracked black pepper
- Pinch salt

INSTRUCTIONS

1. Finely strip the horseradish and cucumber and add to the vinegar, fennel seed, and cardamom pods in a dish.
2. Finely chop the chilli pepper and add to the mix with a pinch of salt and pepper.
3. Finely slice the cabbage.
4. Finely chop the chives and garlic.
5. Heat a pan with 2 tsp oil and put in the prawns, stir for 3–5 mins.
6. Add the garlic and stir for 2 mins.
7. Add the juice from ½ lemon and the wine stir for 2 more min and remove from heat to sit for 4–5 mins.
8. In another hot pan heat the last of the oil and fry the cabbage, season with a pinch of salt and pepper.
9. To serve put the cabbage on the plate and prawns on top, drizzle with the sauce left in the pan and serve the pickle in a dish on the side.

4 portions | 40 mins | 45 mins

Paleo Fish, Chips & Tartar Sauce

INGREDIENTS

- 4 small haddock, cod or Pollock fillets
- 5 eggs
- 75g arrowroot
- 250g ground almonds
- 75ml olive oil
- 2 large sweet potatoes
- 1 girkin
- 1 tsp baby capers or chopped capers
- 1 lemon
- 1 tsp Dijon mustard
- 50ml white wine
- Cracked black pepper
- Sea salt
- Bunch parsley

INSTRUCTIONS

1. First cut the sweet potatoes into chips, toss in a little oil,
2. season well and put on an oven tray in the oven at 180°C for 35 mins.
3. In 3 dishes put the arrowroot, 2 egg beaten and almonds separately.
4. Season the arrowroot with a pinch of salt and pepper and add the fish fillet, then to the egg mix and finally almonds ensuring evenly coated and chill in the fridge for 10–15 mins.
5. For the tartar sauce, blend the yolk of 3 eggs, Dijon, juice of ½ lemon, caper, girkin, wine, 65ml olive oil and pinch of salt and pepper.
6. Finish the sauce with some chopped parsley and chill.
7. Heat the last of the oil and fry the fish for 3 mins each side and finish in the oven a 180°C for 10 mins then serve with the chips and sauce.

4 portions | 20 mins | 40 mins

Smoked Haddock on Wilted Spinach with Celeriac Chips & Poached Egg

INGREDIENTS

- 1 tsp white wine vinegar
- 4 portions smoked haddock
- 80g spinach
- 2 medium celeriac
- 4 eggs
- 2 tbsp olive oil
- Bunch dill
- Cracked black pepper
- Sea salt

INSTRUCTIONS

1. First peel and cut the celeriac into chunky chips and seal in a pan with 1 tsp oil, season well and put in the oven at 190°C for 30 mins.
2. Heat up a pan and with the oil place in the haddock and season with pepper, place the spinach around and put in the oven at 190°C for 8–10 mins.
3. Get a deep pan at hot water with a tsp white wine vinegar, ensuring its hot but not boiling, poach the eggs for 4–5 mins.
4. To serve, stack the chips with the haddock on top and the egg on top of that, place the spinach around and finish with cracked black pepper over the egg.

4 | 25 mins | 30 mins

Baked Trout in Lemon & Parsley with Pan Seared Shredded Vegetables

INGREDIENTS

4 whole small trout

2 lemon

Bunch parsley

2 carrots

1 leek

1 fennel

1 pak choi

1 tbsp olive oil

Cracked black pepper

Sea salt

INSTRUCTIONS

1. Using baking parchment wrap the trout individually with a squeeze of half a lemon on each and season well with salt and pepper.
2. Put in the oven at 200°C for 15–17 then allow to rest.
3. Finely strip the carrots, leek, and fennel and chop the parsley.
4. Using a hot pan, heat the oil and add the carrots and fennel.
5. Cook for 2 mins then add the leek, pak choi and season with a pinch of salt and pepper.
6. To serve place the fish on a plate covering the paper and placing the vegetables on top.
7. Finish with chopped parsley and serve.

notes

Chicken

SWEDEN
adidas

6 | 45 mins | 35 mins

Chicken & Vegetable Skewers with Spiced Rice

INGREDIENTS

Skewers

1 tsp olive oil
3 chicken breasts
1 courgette
2 red onions
2 red peppers
1 medium chilli
½ tsp fennel seeds
½ tsp ground cumin
½ tsp paprika
1 clove garlic coriander

Rice

1 tsp olive oil
2 cauliflowers
1 medium chilli
1 tsp turmeric
½ tsp garam masala
1 small onion
2 bay leaves

INSTRUCTIONS

1. Dice the chicken, courgette, onion and pepper into large chunks.
2. Finely chop the chilli,garlic and coriander.
3. Put the chilli,garlic, coriander, fennel seeds, cumin and paprika into a bowl with the olive oil and mix.
4. Using 6 large skewers push on chicken, courgettes, onion and peppers until it is all on the skewers.
5. Using a large flat oven tray, put the chicken skewers on ensuring they're not touching and with a spoon, drizzle the spice and oil mix over them until they're evenly covered.
6. Cover with cling film and allow to marinade for 1–2 hrs if possible.
7. For the rice, finely chop or grate the cauliflower, finely chop the chilli and onion.
8. Using an oven proof dish ass the cauliflower, oil, chilli, turmeric,garam masala, onion and bay leaves, mix thoroughly and cover with foil.
9. Heat the oven to 200°C and cook chicken for 20 mins.
10. Place the rice in the oven for 15 mins and serve.

6 | 30 mins | 20 mins

Chicken & Chorizo Salad

INGREDIENTS

- 3 chicken breasts
- 250g chopped chorizo
- 1 lime
- Basil
- 200g mixed leaves
- 3 tomatoes
- 1 carrot
- ½ cucumber
- 4 spring onions
- 1 tbsp extra virgin olive oil

INSTRUCTIONS

1. Slice the chicken into thin strips.
2. Finely strip the carrot, cucumber and spring onions.
3. Quarter the tomato taking out the seeds and then finely strip.
4. Using a very hot non-stick pan brown off the chicken.
5. Add the chorizo to the pan and continue to cook for 5–8 mins and allow to rest for 3–4 mins.
6. Using a large bowl place the mixed leaves, tomatoes, carrot, cucumber, spring onion and olive oil and toss.
7. In 6 serving bowls place the salad mix in a spoon on top the chicken and chorizo mix.
8. Finish the dish with a squeeze of lime and serve.

4

40 mins

45 mins

Chicken & Butternut Squash Bake

INGREDIENTS

2 chicken breasts

1 butternut squash

1 onion

1 leek

2 cloves garlic

300ml chicken stock

Thyme

Parsley

50g flaked almonds

Cracked black pepper

Pinch sea salt

INSTRUCTIONS

1. Peel and dice the butternut squash.
2. Dice the chicken, onion and slice the leek.
3. Finely chop the garlic and parsley.
4. In a hot pan brown off the chicken and then add the butternut squash, onion, leeks and garlic and continue to cook.
5. Add the chicken stock and 2 sprigs of thyme and simmer for 10 mins.
6. Season with salt and pepper to taste and pour into an ovenproof dish.
7. Top with flaked almonds and cook in the oven at 160°C for 25 mins ensuring the almonds don't brown.
8. Finish the dish with some chopped parsley and serve.

4 | 50 mins | 60 mins

Pesto Chicken on Sweet Potato, Fennel & Roast Tomatoes

INGREDIENTS

Pesto

1 bunch basil

2 cloves garlic

150ml olive oil

100g pine nuts

Pinch ground black pepper

Pinch salt

INSTRUCTIONS

1. For the pesto, using a blender add the basil leaves,garlic, olive oil and pine nuts. Blend until smooth.
2. Season the mix with salt and pepper to taste.
3. Peel the sweet potato and dice into 1 cm pieces.
4. Slice the fennel and garlic.
5. Quarter the tomatoes.
6. In a hot pan warm the olive oil and put in the sweet potato, fennel and garlic and toss for 2–3 mins season with pepper.
7. Place the mix into a large oven tray and add the tomatoes.
8. Using a hot oven-proof pan seal of the chicken and coat in the pesto and put in the oven at 180°C for 20 minutes.
9. Put the veg in the oven at 180°C for 15 mins.
10. Once done mix the rocket through the roast veg and then serve with the chicken breast on top.

4 | 45 mins | 70 mins

Chicken Pizzaiola

INGREDIENTS

2 large skinless, boneless chicken breasts

1 tin chopped tomatoes

300ml Passata

1 tbsp dried oregano

1 tbsp dried basil

1 tbsp dried parsley

1 tsp rosemary, finely chopped

75ml balsamic vinegar

Fresh chilli to taste

1 onion, finely diced

4 cloves garlic, finely chopped

125g black olives, sliced

2 bell peppers, diced

120g Feta, crumbled

Salt and pepper

Olive oil

INSTRUCTIONS

1. Take the breasts and slice them in half lengthways to create 2 smaller fillets, place these on an oiled roasting sheet and season.
2. Place in the oven at 180°C fan for 20–25 mins until cooked through.
3. In a hot saucepan place the oil, onions and garlic and fry off until softened and lightly browned.
4. Add the herbs chilli and balsamic and mix.
5. Add the tomatoes and passata and reduce to a medium-low heat and allow to simmer for a minimum of 30 mins.
6. Spoon some of the sauce on to the chicken to coat it, and place olives, peppers and feta on top and return to the oven for a further 10–12 mins until peppers are cooked and Feta begins to melt.
7. Serve with salad or roasted Mediterranean vegetables.

4

30 mins

25 mins

Feta & Spinach Stuffed Chicken with Radish and Beetroot Salad

INGREDIENTS

80g feta

40g spinach

4 small chicken breasts

8 salad radish

4 small whole beetroot

1 lemon

100g salad leaves

¼ tsp cracked black pepper

1 tbsp olive oil

INSTRUCTIONS

1. Butterfly chicken breasts.
2. Chop or crumble feta and mix with spinach and pinch black pepper.
3. Stuff the chicken with feta mix and ensure there are nogaps when thicken is wrapped around filling.
4. Season the breasts.
5. Heat up a pan until very hot with the oil and seal the chicken for 2 mins either side and place in an oven at 200°C for 18 mins.
6. Remove and allow to rest for 5 mins.
7. Slice the radish and beetroot into disks and add to salad leaves.
8. Zest ¼ lemon and add to salad mix.
9. Put salad in a bowl and place chicken on top, you can slice if preferred.
10. Using half the lemon finish the dish with squeezing the juice over and serve.

6 | 40 mins | 60 mins

Curried Coconut Chicken & Cauliflower Rice

INGREDIENTS

Curry

600g chicken thighs
2 onions
1 butternut squash
2 cloves garlic
60g spinach
1 tin coconut cream
1 tbsp garam masala
1 tbsp cumin
1 tbsp turmeric
1 tsp paprika
4 medium chillies
Bunch coriander
1 tsp cracked black pepper
2 tin chopped tomatoes

Rice

2 cauliflowers
1 tsp olive oil
Coriander
6 cardamom pods
Cracked black pepper

INSTRUCTIONS

Curry

1. Dice the chicken, onions and butternut squash into 1 cm pieces.
2. Finely chop the garlic and chillies.
3. In a hot large pan brown the diced chicken.
4. Add the onions, butternut squash and garlic and sweat for 5 mins.
5. Add the garam masala, cumin, turmeric, paprika, chilli and black pepper and fry off for 5 mins.
6. Add the chopped tomatoes and simmer for 35 mins.
7. Finish with the coconut cream and chopped coriander.

Rice

1. Finely chop or grate the cauliflower.
2. In an oven proof dish add cauliflower, oil, coriander, cardamom and black pepper.
3. Foil dish and put in oven at 190 degrees C for 20 mins and serve.

4 | 20 mins | 40 mins

Lemon & Thyme Chicken with Roasted Vegetables

INGREDIENTS

2 tbsp olive oil

1 lemon

Small bunch thyme

1 clove garlic

4 small chicken breasts

2 courgettes

1 red pepper

1 yellow pepper

INSTRUCTIONS

1. Marinate the chicken in the zest of 1 lemon, 2–4 sprigs of thyme, chopped garlic and pinch black pepper.
2. Chop the courgettes, red, yellow and green pepper and red onion into 2cm pieces and place in an ovenproof dish
3. Using a very hot pan add a drizzle of olive oil seal off the chicken until golden brown and put in the oven at 170°C for 20 mins.
4. Using a very hot pan and remainder of oil, pan fry all the chopped veg and then add to the oven at 170°C for 12 minutes.
5. Remove chicken and veg and add some thyme leaves to veg and stir.

4 | 60 mins | 30 mins

Chicken & Pepper Enchiladas

INGREDIENTS

Tortilla/Pancake

125g arrowroot

1 egg

1 tsp cold water

Pinch salt

Chicken Filling

2 chicken breasts

1 onion

3 mixed peppers

3 tomatoes

1 tsp honey

1 medium chilli

1 tsp ground cumin

1 tsp paprika

INSTRUCTIONS

1. To make the pancake mix all ingredients together, using a hot non-stick pan pour some of the batter in till base of the pan is coated. Once bubbles appear turn and cook on the other side for 30–60 seconds and allow pancakes to cool.
2. Slice the chicken, onion, peppers, quarter the tomato and finely chop the chilli.
3. Using a hot pan brown off the chicken breast.
4. Add the onion, peppers and chilli and cook for 1–2 mins.
5. Turn down the heat to a medium setting and add the cumin and paprika, cook the mix further for 1–2 mins.
6. Split the mix evenly onto the pancakes and wrap.
7. Put in the oven for 5–8 minutes then serve.
8. It can be served with salad, homemade salsa, cauliflower rice or on its own as a lighter meal.

4

19 mins

40 mins

Sesame chicken on stir fry vegetables

INGREDIENTS

- 4 medium chicken breasts
- 50g sesame seeds
- 20g honey
- Small bunch of coriander
- 1 lime
- 1 green chilli
- 2 cloves of garlic
- 2 pak choi
- 1 red pepper
- 1 red onion
- 1 courgette
- Bunch of spring onions
- 1 tbsp olive oil
- Small pinch of black pepper

INSTRUCTIONS

1. Finely chop the chilli and garlic.
2. Pick the pak choi but leave the leaf intact.
3. Slice the red pepper, onion, courgette, spring onion and coriander.
4. Heat half the oil and add the chicken to colour both sides.
5. Drizzle honey on the chicken and reduce in the pan until very sticky then pour in the sesame seeds coating the chicken evenly.
6. Place in an oven at 170°c for 12 mins.
7. While the chicken cooks, heat the remainder of the oil in a wok. Add the onions, peppers and spring onions and stir fry for 2 mins.
8. Add the chilli,garlic and black pepper and cook for a further 2 mins. Remove from the heat and let sit.
9. Once cooked serve the vegetables on a plate with the chicken on top. Finish with a squeeze of lime and chopped coriander.

4

10 mins

20 mins

Honey and Mustard Chicken

INGREDIENTS

4 small chicken breasts

1 shallot bunch of chives

1 tbsp wholegrain mustard

1 tbsp honey

Pinch salt cracked black pepper

1 tsp olive oil

INSTRUCTIONS

1. In a small hot pan heat half the oil and sweat the sliced shallot for 3 mins.
2. Add the honey and mustard and simmer for 3–4 mins, remove from the heat and add a pinch of black pepper.
3. Heat the remainder of the oil in another pan and seal off the chicken for about 3 mins either side.
4. Add the honey and mustard mix to the chicken and ensure the chicken is evenly coated.
5. Place in an oven at 200°c for 8 mins.
6. Once removed from the oven, allow to rest for 3–5 minutes and finish with chopped chives.
7. To serve – Slice the chicken and serve with salad or steamed vegetables.

4

15 mins

10 mins

Paleo Friendly Red Thai Curry

INGREDIENTS

1 tbsp olive oil

200g chicken breast, diced

2 red bird's eye chillies, roughly chopped

1 thumb sized piece of ginger, peeled and finely chopped

5 kaffir lime leaves (dried or fresh)

1 lemongrass stalk, finely chopped or 1 tsp lemongrass paste

Shallots, peeled and chopped

2 cloves garlic, peeled and finely chopped

1 tsp cumin

1 tsp ground coriander

½ tbsp paprika

1 tbsp fish sauce

Juice of 1 lime

½ tsp of honey

400ml coconut milk (reduced fat, tinned)

INSTRUCTIONS

1. Heat the oil in a large frying pan on a medium-to-high heat. Add the chicken, and cook for 5 minutes until sealed.
2. Whilst the chicken is cooking, place the red chillies, ginger, kaffir lime leaves, lemongrass, shallots, garlic, cumin, ground coriander and paprika into a food processor. Blend until the mixture forms into a paste.
3. Add the paste to the chicken in the pan and cook for 5 minutes, stirring to coat the chicken.
4. Add the fish sauce, lime and honey. Cook for a further 5 minutes, stirring often. By this time the chicken should be cooked through (you can check this by cutting the largest piece of chicken you can find in half and ensuring it's no longer pink in the middle).
5. Add the coconut milk and heat through until almost boiling. Don't let it boil, or it may curdle. If you would like the sauce thicker mix 1 tbsp arrowroot powder with 2 tbsp cold water and stir into the sauce.

Pork

6 40 mins 25 mins

Sage & Onion Sausages

INGREDIENTS

1 pigskin/sausage skin

400g pork mince

2 onions

Sage

¼ tsp nutmeg

Cracked black pepper

Pinch salt

1 clove garlic

INSTRUCTIONS

1. Using a food processor place the onions, small handful sage, nutmeg, pinch black pepper and garlic and blend till quite fine but not smooth.
2. In a bowl add the mince and mix from the food processor.
3. Add a pinch of salt and mix thoroughly.
4. Using a piping bag and round long ended nozzle pipe the meat filling into the skins.
5. Twist the skins to the desired size of sausage and place in the fridge to rest for 1–2 hours if possible.
6. To cook, cut at the twisted area and using a hot non-stick pan brown the sausages and finish in the oven.
7. Or you can frill then serve.

4

40 mins

30 mins

Sweet & Sour Pork with Stir Fried Pak Choi

INGREDIENTS

400g pork loin

1 red onion

1 red pepper

1 green pepper

2 cloves garlic

4 pak choi

Sauce

100g honey

100g tomato puree

500ml white wine vinegar

50ml chicken or vegetable stock

¼ tsp ground black pepper

¼ tsp fennel seeds

⅛ tsp cinnamon

1 star anise

1 clove garlic

1 tbsp arrowroot

INSTRUCTIONS

1. For the sauce – Finely chop the garlic.
2. Using a hot pan sweat of the garlic and then add the fennel seeds, cinnamon, star anise, black pepper and vinegar and simmer for 5 mins.
3. Add the tomato puree and honey and cook for a further 3 mins.
4. Add the chicken stock and simmer for 10 more mins.
5. Add a tsp cold water to the arrowroot and add to the simmering sauce, cook for 5 more mins then pass through a sieve and put to the side.

For the pork:

1. Strip the pork loin.
2. Finely slice the onion, red pepper,green pepper and garlic.
3. Using a hot wok or large frying pan, brown of the pork then add the garlic and onion, cook for 10 mins stirring throughout.
4. Add the green and red peppers, pak choi and cook for 5 more mins stirring throughout.
5. Finish the dish by pouring the sauce over, simmer for 3–5 mins then serve.
6. It can be served with either cauliflower, rice or squash noodles.

4

30 mins

40 mins

Pork Loin Apple & Shallot gravy

INGREDIENTS

4 × 4 oz pork loin steaks

3 large shallots

1 clove garlic

1 large Bramley apple

2 sprigs of thyme

1 tsp olive oil

300ml pork or vegetable stock

1 tsp honey

Cracked black pepper

INSTRUCTIONS

1. Peel and quarter the shallots.
2. Peel and cut the apple into segments.
3. Place the shallots, apple and honey in an oven tray and roast for 25 mins.
4. Roughly chop the garlic and sweat in a hot pan.
5. Add the thyme and stock and leave to simmer.
6. Season the pork steaks with a pinch of black pepper and salt.
7. Using a very hot pan seal of the steaks for 3–4 mins both sides, place on a tray and finish in the oven for 15 mins.
8. Remove the stock from the stove and pass through a sieve.
9. Remove the shallots and apples from the oven and put the tray directly on the heat adding the stock and stirring.
10. Remove the steaks from the oven and spoon the shallot and apple gravy over to serve.
11. This dish can be served with roasted veg, sweet potato ship or sweet potato mash.

4 | 40 mins | 90 mins

Pork, Thyme & Leek Pie

INGREDIENTS

Pastry

400g ground almonds

150g arrowroot

1 egg

1 tbsp olive oil

Pie Filling

500g diced pork

2 leeks

1 onion

1 carrot

Sage

1 clove garlic

500g pork or vegetable stock

1 tsp olive oil

1 tbsp tomato puree

Pinch cracked black pepper

Pinch sea salt

INSTRUCTIONS

1. For the pastry, using a mixing bowl add the almonds, arrowroot, olive oil and 1 egg yolk and mix to a dough and put in the fridge to rest.
2. For the filling, slice and wash the leeks.
3. Finely chop the carrot, onion, sage and garlic.
4. Using a hot pan brown the pork in the olive oil.
5. Add the carrot, leeks, onion and garlic and cook and stir for 10 mins.
6. Add the tomato puree and stock and simmer for 20 mins.
7. Season to taste with salt and pepper, add sage and put in a oven dish.
8. Roll out the pastry using a sprinkle of arrowroot so it doesn't stick.
9. Put in the oven at 160°C for 35–45 mins then serve.

4 | 25 mins | 60 mins

Chilli & Pepper Pork Chop, Sweet Potato Wedges, Roast Peppers & Cherry Tomatoes

INGREDIENTS

- 4 × 4 – 6 oz pork chops
- 2 sweet potatoes
- 1 red pepper
- 1 yellow pepper
- 1 green pepper
- 12 cherry tomatoes
- 2 medium chilli peppers
- 1 tsp pink peppercorns
- 2 tbsp olive oil
- Cracked black pepper
- Chives
- Basil
- Sea salt

INSTRUCTIONS

1. Finely chop the chilli peppers and chives and put over the pork chops.
2. Over the pork pour 1 tbsp oil, add pink peppercorns, pinch black pepper and pinch sea salt and allow to sit in fridge for 15–20 mins.
3. Wash and cut the sweet potato into wedges put in the oven at 180°C for 45 mins.
4. Roughly cut the red, yellow, and green pepper.
5. In an oven tray add the red, yellow and green
6. pepper with the tomatoes, oil, salt and pepper.
7. Put in the oven at 180 degrees for 30 mins.
8. Using a hot pan brown the pork chops and put on an oven tray in the oven at 180°C for 18–20 mins.
9. Serve with torn basil leaves and coriander.

6 | 40 mins | 120 mins

BBQ Ribs

INGREDIENTS

- 2–3 racks pork ribs
- 1.5 ltr vegetable stock
- 10 tomatoes
- 200g tomato puree
- 1 onion
- 2 cloves garlic
- ½ tsp celery salt
- 3–4 tbsps Worcestershire sauce
- 400ml passatta
- 2 tsp English mustard
- 1 tbsp black pepper
- 220g honey
- 2 bay leaves
- 60ml white wine vinegar

INSTRUCTIONS

1. To start put the ribs in a deep oven tray and pour 1 ltr stock over, foil and put in the oven at 190°C for 100 mins.
2. For the sauce finely chop the onion,garlic and tomatoes.
3. Sweat of the onion and garlic in a large pot.
4. Add the vinegar and simmer for 10 mins.
5. Add the tomato puree, tomatoes, stock, celery, salt,
6. Worcestershire sauce, passatta, mustard, black pepper, bay leaves and honey and simmer for 30 mins.
7. Remove bay leaves and blend sauce till smooth no need to sieve.
8. Once ribs are cooled so that they are soft, place on another tray to dry for 3–4 mins then cut to the desired size.
9. Coat in the sauce and put in the oven at 220°C for 15–20 mins then serve.

4 | 30 mins | 120 mins

Pulled Pork with Fennel, Asparagus & Tomato Medley

INGREDIENTS

1 kg pork leg joint

2 ltr pork or vegetable stock

1 bulb garlic

1 tsp black peppercorns

4 bay leaves

2 whole fennel

12 asparagus

4 small bunch vine on cherry plum tomatoes

1 tsp olive oil

Sage

Cracked black pepper

Pinch sea salt

INSTRUCTIONS

1. Using a large hot pan, brown the whole leg in the olive oil.
2. Add the stock, black peppercorns, bay leaves and sage
3. Cut the garlic bulb in half and add to pan and cook for 120 mins on medium heat.
4. For the vegetables slice the fennel and trim the base of the asparagus
5. Using a hot pan, fry the fennel and tomatoes, season with a pinch of black pepper and sea salt.
6. Add the asparagus and roast for 10 mins at 180°C.
7. To serve put the vegetables on a plate and place the pork over, finish with some chopped parsley or chive if wanted.
8. For extra flavour reduce the stock togravy and drizzle.

notes

Vegetarian

ASDA
Organic
EXTRA
VIRGIN
OLIVE
OIL

4

25 mins

25 mins

Ratatouille stuffed aubergine, topped with toasted almonds

INGREDIENTS

1 red onion

3 aubergines

1 red pepper

2 beef tomatoes

2 sprigs of thyme

Small bunch of basil

2 cloves of garlic

1 tbsp tomato puree

20g honey

100g almond flakes

½ tsp cracked black pepper

Pinch of sea salt

INSTRUCTIONS

1. Slice 2 of the aubergines lengthways and hollow out with a spoon leaving 1cm of flesh inside.
2. Finely dice the other aubergine along with the courgette, red pepper, tomatoes and onion and chop the garlic and basil.
3. Using a hot pan, sweat the onions. Add the red pepper, courgettes and garlic after 2 mins and sweat for a further 5 mins.
4. Add the aubergine and tomato and cook for a further 2 mins
5. Add the thyme, basil, tomato puree and ho0ney with a pinch of salt and stir thoroughly.
6. Remove from the heat and spoon the filling evenly into thyme 4 aubergine halves. Top with almond flakes.
7. Cook for 12–15 mins in an oven at 190°C and serve.

6

25 mins

30 mins

Butternut and almond nut roast

INGREDIENTS

- 1 butternut squash
- 1 red onion
- 1 carrot
- 1 clove of garlic
- 1 leek 200g ground almonds
- 1 egg
- 3 sprigs of thyme
- Small bunch of parsley
- ½ tsp cumin
- ½ tsp celery salt
- ½ tsp cracked black pepper
- Pinch of sea salt

INSTRUCTIONS

1. Peel, deseed and finely chop the butternut squash.
2. Finely chop the onion, carrot,garlic and finely slice and wash the leek.
3. Chop the parsley and strip the leaves from the thyme stalks.
4. Using a hot pan, sweat the onion, carrots,garlic, leek and squash for 10 mins and place in a mixing bowl to cool for 10 mins.
5. Add the almonds, egg, thyme, parsley, cumin, celery salt, pepper and a pinch of salt and mix.
6. Place on a sheet of cling film and roll out in the cling film to a thick sausage shape.
7. Using a Bain Marie, put in the oven, covered in foil at 180°C for 25 mins.
8. Remove from the cling film, slice and serve. Can also be served as a larger meal with roast

4 | 60 mins | 20 mins

Stuffed sweet potato with spinach, tomato and a macadamia crust

INGREDIENTS

1 tsp olive oil

2 large sweet potatoes

80g spinach

4 tomato's

1 clove of garlic

Small bunch of chives

1 onion

100g macadamia nuts

½ tsp cracked black pepper

Pinch of sea salt

INSTRUCTIONS

1. Bake the sweet potatoes for 40 mins.
2. Finely chop the tomatoes,garlic, onion and chives.
3. Using a hot pan, heat the oil and sweat the onion and garlic.
4. Add the tomato and chives for 2–3 mins and then remove from the heat.
5. Half the sweet potato lengthways and hollow out the inside.
6. Place sweet potato in a bowl and add the onion,garlic, chives and tomato mix. Finely chop the spinach and add to the mix.
7. Mix thoroughly and season with salt and pepper.
8. Spoon the mix back into the potato skins and top with chopped macadamia nuts.
9. Bake at 190°C for 10 mins and serve.

6

45 mins

45 mins

Root vegetable and rosemary stew

INGREDIENTS

- 4 carrots
- 2 parsnips
- 3 onions
- 2 sweet potato
- 2 leeks
- 500g chestnut mushrooms
- 1 clove of garlic
- Small bunch of rosemary
- 2 tbsp olive oil
- 125g of Arrowroot
- 1 egg
- 1 litre vegetable stock
- ½ tsp cracked black pepper
- Pinch of sea salt

INSTRUCTIONS

1. Wash the veg and chop the carrots, sweet potato, parsnips and onion into 1cm cubes
2. Slice the leeks into 1cm think pieces and wash.
3. Finely chop the garlic
4. Using a hot pan, sweat the onions and garlic in 1 tbsp of oil for 5 mins then add the carrots, parsnips, potato and leek. Cook for a further 5 mins stirring regularly.
5. Add the stock and a few sprigs of rosemary, bring to the boil and then simmer for 35 mins.
6. For the dumplings
7. Finely chop the mushroom, place on a tray and roast in the oven for 10 mins with a few sprigs of rosemary.
8. Place the mushrooms in a bowl and add the arrowroot, the last of the oil, 1 egg and salt and pepper. Mix thoroughly and form into 6 even sized balls.
9. Place the balls on top of the stew for the last 10 mins of cooking and cover.
10. To serve, remove the dumplings, season the stew well and scoop into bowls with a dumpling placed on top.

4 | 20 mins | 35 mins

Aubergine and mixed pepper gratin

INGREDIENTS

1 tsp olive oil

2 aubergines

1 red pepper

1 yellow pepper

1 green pepper

1 onion

2 plum tomatoes

1 tbsp tomato puree

200ml vegetable stock

1 clove of garlic

Small bunch of thyme

150g of feta cheese

½ tsp cracked black pepper

Pinch of sea salt

INSTRUCTIONS

1. Slice the aubergine into 4mm thick discs
2. Slice the peppers and onion into large pieces and thinly slice the tomatoes.
3. Finely chop the garlic.
4. In a hot pan, sweat the garlic in a little oil.
5. Add the tomato puree, stock and a few sprigs of thyme and simmer.
6. In an oven tray, put the peppers, onion and aubergine and roast for 15 mins at 160°C.
7. Remove from the tray and put in an ovenproof dish.
8. Pour over the sauce and top with sliced tomatoes.
9. Crumble the feta on top and bake at 160°C for 25 mins.
10. Finish with cracked black pepper and serve.

4 | 30 mins | 25 mins

Layered aubergine with courgette, shallot, rocket & basil

INGREDIENTS

1 tsp olive oil
2 aubergines
2 courgettes
6 large shallots
60g rocket
8 basil leaves
1 tbsp tomato puree
2 sprigs of thyme
Cracked black pepper
250ml passatta
20g honey
Pinch of sea salt
1 clove of garlic

INSTRUCTIONS

1. Slice the aubergine and courgette 4–5mm thick.
2. Peel and slice the shallots and garlic.
3. Dry roast the aubergine and courgette in the oven at 180°C for 10 mins and then allow to cool.
4. Heat the oil in a pan and sweat the shallots and garlic.
5. Add the tomato puree, thyme, honey, passatta along with the salt and pepper.
6. Shred the basil and rocket and add to the pan.
7. In an ovenproof dish, place a layer the aubergine and courgette followed by a layer of shallot mix and repeat until all the ingredients have been used, ensuring you finish with a layer of shallot mix.
8. Place in the oven at 200°C for 10 mins.garnish with a little rocket or basil and serve.

6 15 mins 90 mins

Spiced Sweet Potato, Spinach & Cashew Casserole

INGREDIENTS

- 1 tbsp tomato puree
- 60g Cashew nuts
- 1 large onion
- 100g Spinach
- 2 cloves of garlic
- small bunch of coriander
- 1 tbsp garam masala
- 1 tbsp turmeric
- 1 tbsp cumin
- 1 tbsp paprika
- 400ml vegetable stock
- Pinch of cracked black pepper
- 1 tsp Olive Oil

INSTRUCTIONS

1. Peel and dice both the sweet potato and onion and finely chop the garlic
2. Heat the olive oil in a large pan
3. Then sweat off the onions for 10 mins before adding the sweet potato and garlic.
4. Cook for a further 10–12 mins stirring occasionally and adding the spices after 5 mins and the tomato puree after a further 5 mins and cook for another 2 mins.
5. Add stock and garlic and season with black pepper.
6. Transfer the mixture into an ovenproof casserole dish, sprinkle with the cashews, cover and place in a preheated oven at 160°c for 60 mins.
7. Serve garnished with coriander.

6 | 10 mins | 90 mins

Spiced Sweet Potato, Spinach & Cashew Casserole

INGREDIENTS

1 tbsp tomato puree

60g Cashew nuts

1 large onion

100g Spinach

2 cloves of garlic

small bunch of coriander

1 tbsp garam masala

1 tbsp turmeric

1 tbsp cumin

1 tbsp paprika

400ml vegetable stock

Pinch of cracked black pepper

1 tsp Olive Oil

INSTRUCTIONS

1. Peel and dice both the sweet potato and onion and finely chop the garlic
2. Heat the olive oil in a large pan then sweat off the onions for 10 mins before adding the sweet potato and garlic. Cook for a further 10–12 mins stirring occasionally and adding the spices after 5 mins and the tomato puree after a further 5 mins and cook for another 2 mins.
3. Add stock and garlic and season with black pepper.
4. Transfer the mixture into an ovenproof casserole dish, sprinkle with the cashews, cover and place in a preheated oven at 160°c for 60 mins.
5. Serve garnished with coriander.

4

20 mins

90 mins

Vegetable Lasagne

INGREDIENTS

1 Butternut squash

1 Courgette

1 Onion

3 Plum tomatoes

1 Carrot

1 tbsp tomato puree

2 Cloves garlic

200ml vegetable stock

Small bunch of basil

20g feta cheese

50g Spinach

1 tsp Olive oil

Cracked black pepper

INSTRUCTIONS

1. Finely dice the carrot, onion and garlic.
2. Dice the courgette and tomatoes.
3. To act as the 'lasagne sheets – top, tail, peel and deseed the squash and thinly slices lengthways.
4. Shred the basil and spinach.
5. Sweat the onions and carrots in a hot pan for 5 mins then add the garlic and chopped tomatoes. Cook for a further 5 mins.
6. Add the courgettes, tomato puree, stock and a pinch of black pepper and simmer for 5 mins then stir in the basil and spinach.
7. In a large ovenproof dish, layer the sauce with squash with at least 3 layers.
8. Crumble feta on top and bake at 160°c for approx. 50 mins until the squash is soft when stabbed with a knife.

4 | 10 mins | 30 mins

Egg, Asparagus and Avocado Salad

INGREDIENTS

- 4 eggs
- 12 asparagus spears
- 2 avocados
- 50g watercress
- 50g rocket
- 4 salad tomatoes
- 1 red onion
- 1 tbsp extra virgin olive oil
- Pinch of cracked black pepper

INSTRUCTIONS

1. Hard boil, cool and peel the eggs and cut into quarters.
2. Blanch the asparagus for 90 seconds in boiling water then refresh in cold water until completely cooled.
3. With the flesh from avocado dice into small pieces.
4. Quarter the tomatoes, peel and slice the onion.
5. Put the watercress, rocket, tomatoes, onion and asparagus in a bowl and toss together with olive oil.

To Serve – Place a hand full of salad mix on the plate then place 4 quarters of the egg on top and sprinkle with avocado and a pinch of cracked black pepper.

Soups

TEAM

6 | 20 mins | 45 mins

Tomato & Basil

INGREDIENTS

1 large onion

2 sticks celery

3 clove garlic

2 carrots

200g tomato puree

10 tomatoes

500ml vegetable stock

1 bunch basil

1 tsp cracked black pepper

30g honey

INSTRUCTIONS

1. Roughly chop onion, celery, carrots,garlic and tomatoes.
2. Heat a large pan and sweat of the onion, celery, carrots and garlic.
3. Add the roughly chopped tomatoes and tomato puree stirring continuously.
4. Add honey, passatta and stock and simmer for 25 mins.
5. Blend mix until smooth.
6. Pass through a sieve.
7. Finely chop basil and add to soup.
8. Add pepper to taste before serving.

6 | 30 mins | 60 mins

Spiced Butternut Squash & Spinach

INGREDIENTS

- 2 butternut squash
- 1 large onion
- 2 cloves garlic
- 600ml vegetable stock
- 60g spinach
- ½ tsp nutmeg
- 1 tsp cumin
- 2 stick celery
- Pinch sea salt and cracked black pepper

INSTRUCTIONS

1. Peel, de-seed and roughly chop butternut squash.
2. Roughly chop onion,garlic and celery.
3. Heat up a large pan and add onions,garlic, celery and butternut squash and sweat off for 5 mins.
4. Add nutmeg and cumin and stir for 2 mins.
5. Add stock and simmer for 40 mins.
6. Add spinach and take off the heat and leave for 5 mins.
7. Blend soup until smooth, it won't need sieved.
8. Season with salt and pepper to taste and serve.

6 | 30 mins | 60 mins

Chicken, Leek & Watercress

INGREDIENTS

2 chicken breasts

2 leeks

50g watercress

2 onion

1 clove garlic

1 ltr chicken stock

½ tsp cracked black

Small bunch thyme

Pinch sea salt

INSTRUCTIONS

1. Place chicken breasts in a ovenproof dish and pour 200ml of stock over them and place into an oven at 190°C for 25 mins. When done, allow to cool.
2. Finely chop the chicken and leeks and place to one side.
3. Roughly chop the onion and garlic.
4. Using a large pan on a medium heat sweat off the onions and garlic.
5. Add 2 sprigs of thyme and stock, simmer for 30 mins.
6. Take off the heat and blend until smooth.
7. Pass the mix through a sieve.
8. Add the watercress and blend again.
9. Add the black pepper and chicken and return to heat for 5 more mins.
10. Wash the leeks and drain.
11. Pan fry the leeks until crispy but not dark in colour.
12. Season the soup to taste.
13. When serving top the soup with the crispy leeks as a garnish.

6

30 mins

90 mins

Lamb & Vegetable

INGREDIENTS

300g lamb leg

1 onion

1 stick celery

2 carrots

½ swede

1 butternut squash

2 leeks

1 ltr vegetable or lamb stock

1 clove garlic

Small bunch rosemary

½ tsp cracked black pepper

Pinch sea salt

INSTRUCTIONS

1. Finely dice the lamb, onion, celery, carrots, swede, leeks, butternut squash and garlic
2. In a hot large pan brown off the lamb.
3. Add the onion, celery, carrot, swede, leeks, butternut squash and garlic and continue to stir for 5 more mins.
4. Add the stock and rosemary and simmer for 60–80 mins.
5. Remove the rosemary stalks.
6. Add black pepper and remove from heat.
7. Season with sea salt to taste before serving.

6

35 mins

60 mins

Carrot & Coriander

INGREDIENTS

800g carrots

2 onions

1 stick of celery

900ml vegetable stock

1 bunch of coriander

½ tsp cracked black pepper

Pinch of salt

1 tsp extra virgin olive oil

INSTRUCTIONS

1. Roughly chop carrots, celery, onions and garlic.
2. In a large hot pot sweat off carrots, celery, onions and garlic in the olive oil.
3. Add the stock and allow to simmer for 45 mins.
4. Blend soup until smooth.
5. Pass the soup through a strainer.
6. Add the coriander and blend again and add the black pepper.
7. Allow to simmer for 5 mins and season with sea salt to taste before serving.

8 20 mins 90 mins

Beef and Tomato Soup

INGREDIENTS

- 125g diced beef or minced beef
- 100g tomato puree
- 4 plum tomatoes
- 1 onion
- 1 clove of garlic
- 1 carrot
- 800ml beef stock
- Small bunch of basil
- Pinch of cracked black pepper
- 1 tsp of olive oil

INSTRUCTIONS

1. Heat the oil in a large pan and add the beef and stir until brown.
2. Roughly chop the onion, carrot, tomatoes and garlic, add to the beef and continue to cook while stirring for 10–15 mins.
3. Add the tomatoes and tomato puree to the mix and stir.
4. Add the stock and simmer for 60 mins.
5. Once the beef is soft use a blender to blend the soup until thick and smooth.
6. Season with pepper and finish with shredded basil to serve.

Sauces

6

10 mins

2 hr

Stock/Gravy 6 portions

INGREDIENTS

300g carrots

1 bulb garlic

1 large leek

2 onions

300–400g meat offcuts or bones

1 tsp tomato puree

2 sprigs thyme

INSTRUCTIONS

1. Roast off any bones or offcuts of meat until dark in colour
2. Roughly chop the carrot, leek, onions and then wash the leeks
3. In a large pan brown off the vegetables
4. Add the browned bones/meat,garlic and thyme
5. After 1 hour add tomato puree
6. After 2 hours strain the stock and it's ready to use

6 portions

15 mins

25 mins

Sweet and Sour Sauce

INGREDIENTS

100g honey

100g tomato puree

50ml white wine vinegar

50ml fresh chicken or vegetable stock

¼ tsp ground black pepper

¼ tsp fennel seeds

⅛ tsp cinnamon

1 star anise

1 clove garlic

1 tbsp arrowroot

INSTRUCTIONS

1. Finely chop the garlic
2. Sweat of in a pan gently you don't want to colour it
3. Add the vinegar and reduce for 5 mins on a low heat
4. Add the honey, tomato puree, stock, fennel seeds, cinnamon, star anise and simmer for 5–10 mins
5. In a separate jug add the arrowroot with 1 tsp water and stir till dissolved
6. Slowly add the arrowroot mix to the sauce whisking continuously
7. Allow to simmer for 5 more mins
8. Add black pepper to taste then serve

n/a

15 mins

90 mins

Tomato Ketchup

INGREDIENTS

10 tomatoes

200g tomato purée

400ml passatta

2 cloves

1 onion

½ tsp celery salt

¼ tsp Worchester sauce

½ ground black pepper

200g honey

INSTRUCTIONS

1. Chop the onions and tomatoes 1 cm thick
2. Sweat of in a large pan
3. Add tomato purée, passatta, cloves, celery salt, Worchester sauce, honey and black pepper
4. Simmer for 90 minutes
5. Blend until smooth
6. Pass through a sieve and allow to cool overnight before serving

n/a | 25 mins | 90 mins

BBQ Sauce

INGREDIENTS

- 60ml white wine vinegar
- 10 tomatoes
- 200g tomato purée
- 1 onion
- 2 cloves garlic
- 2 cloves
- ½ tsp celery salt
- 3 tbsps Worchester sauce
- 400ml passatta
- 1 tsp mustard (English)
- ½ tsp black pepper
- 200g honey
- 2 bay leaves

INSTRUCTIONS

1. Roughly chop the tomatoes, onion and garlic
2. In a hot pan brown of onions then add garlic and tomatoes
3. Add the vinegar, tomato purée, cloves, celery salt, passatta, Worchester sauce, mustard, honey and bay leaves
4. Allow to simmer for 90 mins
5. Remove bay leaves and cloves
6. Blend until smooth
7. Pass through a sieve
8. Allowed to rest overnight before serving

6 portions

10 mins

10 mins

Dairy Free Hollandaise

INGREDIENTS

4 egg yolks

1 tsp white wine vinegar

1 tsp lemon juice

100ml extra-virgin olive oil

1 bay leaf

INSTRUCTIONS

1. Separate the eggs as the whites are not needed
2. Put the yolks, vinegar, lemon juice and bay leaf in a metal bowl on a Bain Marie and whisk continuously for 30–60 seconds
3. Slowly drizzle the oil into the mix while whisking
4. When at a nice consistency remove bay leaves
5. The sauce should be thick enough to coat the back of a spoon and it's ready to serve

n/a n/a n/a

Spiralled Carrots

INGREDIENTS
Carrots
Olive oil
Rosemary

INSTRUCTIONS

1. Preheat oven to 180 degrees C.
2. Spiralize the carrots using an electric machine or hand operated.
3. Place spiralized carrots in an oven tray.
4. Spray olive oil over carrots.
5. Sprinkle rosemary over carrots.
6. Place in oven at 180 degrees C for 15–20 mins until they have soften as much as desired.

n/a n/a n/a

Tahini Yoghurt Dressing

(Perfect jazz up a chicken salad!)

INGREDIENTS	INSTRUCTIONS
Natural full fat yoghurt	1. Chop, chop, chop, mix, mix, mix. Job done!
Garlic, chopped	
Coriander, chopped	
Cucumber, chopped	

notes

Accompaniments

4 | 15 mins | 10 mins

TEAM Sunday Lunch Trimmings: Stuffing

INGREDIENTS

- 3½ cups onion, diced
- 2½ cups celery, diced
- 1 cup apple, cored and diced
- ¼ cup dates, chopped into small pieces
- 2 cups almond flour
- 2 tsps sage
- 2 tsps thyme
- ¼ tsp marjoram
- ¼ tsp rosemary
- ¼ tsp pepper
- ½ tsp salt
- 2 tbsps butter, ghee or coconut oil
- 3 whisked eggs

INSTRUCTIONS

1. Preheat your oven to 175°C and grease a medium-sized baking dish.
2. Add 2 tbsps butter, ghee or coconut oil to a saucepan and warm over low/medium heat.
3. Add the onion, celery, apple and herbs and sauce over medium heat for 5 minutes and then remove from heat.
4. In a large bowl, add the almond flour and dates and mix well.
5. Add the lightly beaten eggs to the bowl and combine it all together.
6. Tip the mixture to baking dish and cook for 45 minutes – 1 hour.

4 | 20 mins | 20 mins

TEAM's World Famous Paleo Yorkshire Pudding

INGREDIENTS

3 large eggs

½ cup milk or non-dairy alternative

½ cup arrowroot starch

¼ cup butter melted and divided (or use meat juices or coconut oil)

½ tsp salt

INSTRUCTIONS

1. Preheat oven to 200°C with yorkshire pudding tins inside the oven to preheat as well.
2. Combine the eggs, milk, arrowroot starch, sea salt and ⅛ cup melted butter and mix into make a thin batter.
3. Lightly drizzle the remaining ⅛ cup melted butter into the hot yorkshire pudding tins and then return to the oven for 3–5 minutes or until butter is sizzling.
4. Remove tray with sizzling butter carefully from the oven and pour in the batter distributing it evenly, otherwise people will fight over the biggest one!
5. Bake for 15–20 minutes. They will puff up and brown at the edges while the centre will be softer but set.

4 | 15 mins | 10 mins

Almond Bread

INGREDIENTS

1½ cups almond flour

½ cup arrowroot

½ tsp sea salt

½ tsp baking powder

¼ tsp garlic powder (optional)

1 tsp apple cider vinegar

3 eggs

1 tbsp coconut oil

INSTRUCTIONS

1. Place the dry ingredients in a bowl and mix well.
2. Put the vinegar eggs and melted coconut oil in a bowl and whisk together.
3. Add the wet to the dry ingredient gradually until a smooth sticky dough is formed.
4. Add the mixture to a well lined loaf tin and place in a preheated oven at 170°C fan.
5. Bake for 30–40 minutes until a skewer comes out clean and the bread has a nice bounce.
6. You can also spoon the mixture onto a baking sheet to make bread rolls.

notes

Printed in Poland
by Amazon Fulfillment
Poland Sp. z o.o., Wrocław

90596503R00096